REMEMBERING
SOUTH CAPE MAY

REMEMBERING
SOUTH CAPE MAY

The Jersey Shore Town That
Vanished into the Sea

JOSEPH G. BURCHER
with ROBERT KENSELAAR

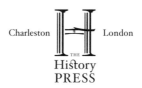

Charleston   London

THE
History
PRESS

Published by The History Press

Charleston, SC 29403

www.historypress.net

First published 2010. Second printing 2010. Manufactured in the United States

ISBN 978.1.59629.314.4

Library of Congress Cataloging-in-Publication Data

Burcher, Joseph G., 1923-

Remembering South Cape May : the Jersey shore town that vanished into the sea / Joseph G. Burcher with Robert Kenselaar.

p. cm.

Includes bibliographical references and index.

ISBN 978-1-59629-314-4

1. South Cape May (N.J. : Borough)--History. 2. South Cape May (N.J. : Borough)--Biography. 3. Burcher, Joseph G., 1923---Homes and haunts. 4. Lower (N.J. : Township)--History. I. Kenselaar, Robert. II. Title.

F144.S625B87 2010

974.9'98--dc22

2010021981

Contents

CONTENTS

Foreword

S outh Cape May—a separate little borough founded in 1894 that completely vanished in about half a century—has long held a fascination for both Cape May area vacationers and lifelong residents like me. In this book, Joseph G. Burcher lays out South Cape May's history from a very personal perspective, as someone who lived there—one of its last surviving residents—and as someone whose family history is closely intertwined with the borough's. Edgar Francis Burcher Sr., Joe's father, served as the last borough clerk of South Cape May. At one time, Joe's family owned three houses in the borough, including one his grandfather had built in 1923, the year that Joe was born.

To give a very quick summary of South Cape May's history: it sprang up at the tail end of the nineteenth century on a small patch of beachfront about a mile long. Some years earlier, that spot lay right at the foot of what was called the largest hotel in the world, the Mount Vernon—although it's not exactly clear where that hotel sat, since it burned completely to the ground in 1856, never fully built. A few years before it was officially incorporated as a municipality, South Cape May itself was known as Mount Vernon, and its earliest development included trolley tracks running right along the beach, a forty-foot-high building in the shape of an elephant and several striking homes that were designed by the most prominent architect in Cape May's history, Stephen Decatur Button.

As a municipality, South Cape May's total lifespan was just fifty-one years, officially ceasing as a separate borough in 1945. During that time, South

FOREWORD

Cape May weathered storms, nor'easters and major hurricanes, its beach drastically eroding, until all of its homes were either moved, abandoned or destroyed. Some time afterward, the former borough was a pasture for a small herd of cattle, and finally, in 1981, it became a nature preserve known as South Cape May Meadows, owned by the Nature Conservancy, with a sizable colony of piping plovers and other birds.

The South Cape May home that Joe Burcher remembers most fondly—where he spent the summers of his boyhood and young adult years—was originally built in 1893 and destroyed in a hurricane in the 1940s. Two other homes owned by his family were among the last standing at the original site of South Cape May in the early '50s. A final storm came along and knocked those little cottages off their foundations, and Joe's family moved them north to the other side of Sunset Boulevard in West Cape May.

Part of Joe's father's job as clerk was to write up the minutes of the borough council, tracking the council's business and, in a sense, the history of South Cape May. Joe and Bob Kenselaar have taken up and expanded on that responsibility here to set down a record of the borough. If you dig deep enough, as they have, there's plenty of information about South Cape May to be found—at the Cape May County Historical and Genealogical Society, the New Jersey State Archives, the Archives of the Cape May County Clerk and the Athenaeum of Philadelphia, as well as in the pages of the *Cape May Star and Wave* and its predecessors. This book draws from these sources and from memories, too.

Half of the book is devoted to Joe's own recollections of living in South Cape May, with plenty of detail about everyday life in South Cape May and nearby from the 1920s onward, wonderfully representative of family life in the Cape May area years ago. Joe also shares his view of South Cape May's aftermath, as seen from his summer cottage on Sunset Boulevard—looking out on the South Cape May Meadows preserve, where bird-watchers from all over flock throughout the year. Joe tells me he's about 150 feet from the path that was once Ninth Avenue in South Cape May, which makes a straight shot to the beach near where he and his eleven brothers and sisters spent the summers of their youth.

The borough of South Cape May itself is gone, but here we have its history and the stories of one of its last living residents.

Robert W. Elwell Sr.
Former Mayor, City of Cape May
Columnist, "Days Gone By," *Cape May Star and Wave*

8

Acknowledgements

This book began as a conversation between my father-in-law, Joe Burcher, and me one night in his summer cottage on Sunset Boulevard in West Cape May. Over the next few days, we continued talking while hiking to the ocean where South Cape May once stood and driving around Joe's old area haunts. I followed up with interviews with others in the family and trips to archives and libraries. I brought the historical material and interview transcripts together to form this book, with Joe's narrative voice.

I'm grateful to Joe for working with me on this project and especially grateful to him and his wife, Vida, for bringing their wonderful daughter Bonnie, the love of my life, into the world.

Joe and I would like to acknowledge Pary Woehlcke and Sonia Forry of the Cape May County Historical and Genealogical Society and the staff of other repositories noted in the foreword by Bob Elwell, who also helped greatly. Special thanks to the authors of outstanding works on the history of the area, Emil R. Salvini, Joe J. Jordan and Jeffrey M. Dorwart, and also to Jim Campbell, Barbara Bergeron and Tom Dvorschak.

Robert Kenselaar

PART I

The Early History to the 1920s

CHAPTER 1

From the Lenni Lenapes
to an Elephant

THE MEADOWS, INDIANS, PIRATES AND PILGRIMS

The two-square-mile bit of land that was once the borough of South Cape May is now known simply as "the Meadows," and it has the look and feel of what the whole region was like long before civilization. The great naturalist Witmer Stone, in his classic two-volume work *Bird Studies at Old Cape May*, writes regretfully of the conditions of South Cape May in 1937 but poetically about the beauty of the surroundings it once mirrored, and he imagines what the wider region was like before the nineteenth century:

> *There is a charm about the meadows at all seasons whether they are clad in the green of summer, with still blue waterways interspersed, or wrapped in the dull brown of midwinter, with channels and ponds ice-bound. It is in spring, however, that they especially appeal to me, when the mainland is bright with opening buds and everywhere tinted with green and crimson but the meadows still apparently in the grip of winter with scarcely a sign of spring vegetation. To offset this, however, they are all astir with the hosts of migrating shore birds and with flocks of gulls and terns en route to their breeding grounds...*
>
> *Picture to yourself beach after beach, along the coast with the surf rolling in just as it does today but in place of the lines of hotels and cottages, the boardwalks and electric lights, fishing piers and throngs of*

bathers, we see only an endless stretch of gleaming strand flanked by sand dunes capped with beach grass—and behind these, sometimes partly buried by them, dense thickets of cedar, scrub oak, wild cherry, holly, and sumac.[1]

The pre-nineteenth-century history of the area that became South Cape May is, essentially, the history of the Cape May region overall, well known to local residents. In the early twentieth century, South Cape May residents, such as my family and I, were well aware of the connection of the borough's land with early Indian residents. While developing Sunset Boulevard in South Cape May during the summer of 1926, road workers excavated part of the old Reeves farm and found burial grounds and artifacts of the Kechemeche tribe of the Lenni Lenapes. The Kechemeches had villages in the area and a sophisticated network of trails. They cultivated corn and vegetables and hunted game, which included giant turkeys and huge bison, according to one early explorer's account. As young children, my brothers and sisters and neighborhood friends would imagine Indians walking along the beach and hunting deer in the brush, especially by Cape Island Creek, which formed the eastern border of our borough.[2]

We also knew of the early European explorers, such as Henry Hudson, sailing in the area that became known as Delaware Bay aboard his ship, the *Half Moon*, anchoring near Cape May Point on August 28, 1609. It's likely that he and his crew gazed on the South Cape May beach west of there before moving on to explore what became New York Harbor and the Hudson River. Hudson, an Englishman sailing for the Dutch, was soon followed by other explorers from the Netherlands, including Captain Cornelius Jacobsen Mey, who sailed to Manhattan Island in 1623 aboard his ship the *Good Tidings*. Mey also ventured south and named the Delaware Bay peninsula Cape Mey. About that same time, Mey was appointed by the Dutch West India Company as the first director of New Netherlands, the colonial area claimed by the Dutch that extended from Cape Cod to the area of New York, New Jersey and south to the Delmarva Peninsula.[3]

The Europeans' encounters with Indians are well documented. In 1630, representatives of the Dutch West India Company purchased a sixteen-square-mile tract of land from a group of ten Indians that apparently included what later became South Cape May—from the east side of Cape May Point stretching four miles northward and spanning four miles eastward along the shore, past where most of Cape May City sits today. The Dutch never established a permanent settlement in the Cape May area, though, and in the 1660s, they ceded New Netherlands to the English.

The first permanent European settlers in the Greater Cape May area came later in the century. They also purchased land from the Indians, signing a deed with a leader named Panktoe in 1687. These settlers were whalers from New England and Long Island who migrated south in the summer season, founding a town on the Delaware Bay known by a number of names: New England Town, Portsmouth, Cape May Town or simply Town. Whaling died out in the area before long, and the settlers turned to farming and fishing.

Among the signers of that 1687 deed with Panktoe was Joseph Whilldin, who appears to have had a direct connection with South Cape May's land—or, at least, his family name was connected. Whilldin's name was also variously spelled Weldon, Welden or Whilldon, and records show that two hundred acres that he owned in the late seventeenth century were situated in the general area that became South Cape May. Even more evidence of his family's connection is found in mid-nineteenth-century maps of the South Cape May area. One 1850 map clearly shows the area later known as South

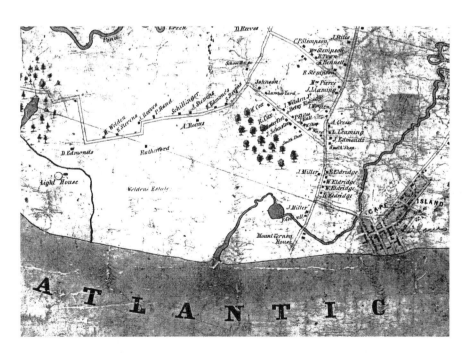

From *The Borough of Cape Island and Its Vicinity*, P. Nunan, 1850. *Courtesy of City of Cape May, Historic Preservation Commission.*

Cape May as largely part of the "Welden Estate." Another map from the period identifies Isaac Whilldin as the owner (through 1849) of part of the beachfront west of Seventh Avenue that became South Cape May.[4]

Overall, though, among the historical figures in the Cape May area during the seventeenth and early eighteenth centuries, the ones who resounded especially with my brothers and me as children were Captain Kidd and Blackbeard, the notorious pirates. According to our own family lore, our grandfather himself came from a line of pirates based in the Caribbean, although I found out later he was actually from Bermuda. It's well documented that William Kidd visited the New Jersey shore along his journey from the Caribbean to New York and Boston, and Cape May was well known in his day as a good place to stop off for fresh water from the small lakes and ponds close to the ocean. The local rumors were that Kidd and his men had buried treasure somewhere around Davey's Lake, not far from Sunset Boulevard. Edward Teach, known as Blackbeard, was also known to have sailed through Cape May coastal shipping routes, and local legend had it that he buried treasure in Cape May, too, although he spent much more time around the Carolinas. Sometimes we'd dig in the sand, thinking we'd find those treasures ourselves someday. The Cape May area still holds a little treasure hunt for children on the beach every year, with a Captain Kidd pirate theme.

In 1726, the first census of the major Cape May settlement—then known as Cape Island—showed 668 residents. Among them were the Eldredges, who, like the Whilldins and many early Cape May settlers, were descended from passengers who sailed on the *Mayflower*. Ezekiel Eldredge, in fact, was another signer of the 1687 deed with Panktoe. Homes owned by both the Whilldin family (built sometime before 1720) and the Eldredge family (built in 1780) still stand today, both on Broadway in West Cape May, within two blocks of each other and less than a mile from South Cape May. Members of the Eldredge family eventually lived for a time in South Cape May in the early twentieth century.

In the early 1800s, not long after the Eldredges built that house on Broadway, development in the area overall increased quite a bit as a result of the regular journeys to the Cape by summer vacationers aboard sailing sloops from Philadelphia. By the mid-nineteenth century, Cape Island was a prominent seaside resort, thanks to its easy access by ship—from Baltimore as well as Philadelphia—and its gently sloping, sandy beaches.

The Mount Vernon House and Hotel

In the early 1800s, there was still only modest development in Cape Island, as noted by one writer about a Fourth of July trip there in 1841: "Cape Island proper is a narrow strip of land of less than half a mile in width, bounding on the sea...in many parts not more than ten or twelve feet wide." He described the village as "a showy little place, the houses being all whitewashed or painted with red roofs." Out of about fifty dwellings, four were hotels, along with three or four private boardinghouses, "closely huddled together, not more than a hundred yards from the sea shore." One of the four hotels was an exception, the Mount Vernon House, situated to the west near Cape Island Creek, which later formed the border between Cape May City and South Cape May.

> *The "Mount Vernon House" stands alone, in the country as it were, some three or four hundred yards from the village, and at this distance more resembles a large farm mansion than a hotel...Being some considerable distance farther removed from the surf than the others it can receive but little patronage, I think, other than that given it by invalids and such as desire only the benefits to be derived from a sea air. It is retired and free from the bustle that hangs about all the others.*[5]

The site of the Mount Vernon House—just past the border of the area that became South Cape May—would later become important in the borough's history.

In 1852, a group of investors from Philadelphia and South Jersey, led by John West, formed the Mount Vernon Hotel Company to build what was touted as the largest hotel in the world. Even before completion, its costs came to $125,000, and among its principal investors was Marcus Aurelius Root, an important figure in the history of photography, who owned one of the nation's largest daguerreotype studios. The hotel was situated in the same general area as the Mount Vernon House, the consensus of historical opinion placing it near the beach at the west end of Cape May, just west of Broadway. Some two hundred people were employed in building the hotel by May 1852. Construction was well underway by July 1853, when 250 feet of the roof were ripped off by the wind in a severe storm, the rain pouring down in torrents. Although it was unoccupied at that time, the hotel was in operation later that season, hosting a concert and a dance in August in

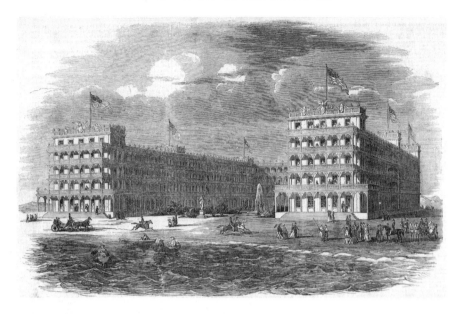

Mount Vernon Hotel, from the *Illustrated London News*, September 17, 1853. *Courtesy of the New York Public Library.*

its large dining hall, 425 feet by 60 feet, with forty gas-burning chandeliers aglow in a huge dining hall.

The *Illustrated London News* published an engraving in September 1853 showing how the hotel would appear when completed and described it as entirely finished. Overstating the hotel's features considerably, the article claimed the building had 3,500 rooms and was always full. The builders were actually planning to have 1,200 rooms, housing 3,000 guests, but by the opening of the summer season in 1854, hotel construction was only far enough along to accommodate 700 guests, a number that grew to 1,000 for the 1855 season and to 2,100 in 1856. That 1856 season started out with booming business for the hotel—more than 7,000 guests had visited by the end of July—but it ended in disaster on September 5, when the entire building burned to the ground in less than two hours, according to newspaper accounts. "The flames darted along the building from wall to wall, through the long saloon over 400 feet long and up the high towers, till it presented one vast sheet of fire that illuminated the surrounding space for miles." Wood shavings and building rubbish from the still-uncompleted all-wood structure had been stashed between the first floor and the ground, making for tinderbox-like conditions. As it was somewhat late in the summer season,

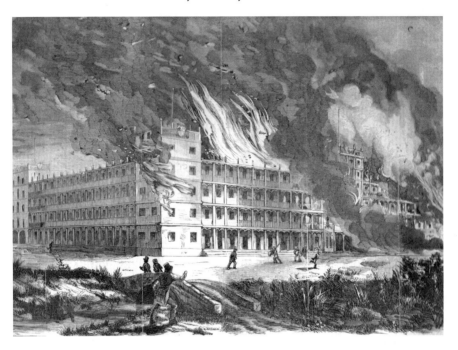

Mount Vernon Hotel in flames. September 20, 1856, *Frank Leslie's Illustrated Newspaper.*

there were no guests at the hotel at the time, but one of the proprietors, Philip Cain, four of his children and a housekeeper were there, and all died. There was an arson suspect: "an Irish woman, who had formerly been engaged in the family as a domestic…went to the Mount Vernon…and demanded a balance of four dollars and fifty cents that was due her." Put off by the family, she "threatened to send them to h–ll." She was arrested but ultimately released for lack of evidence. Early accounts reported that the hotel was uninsured, but later reports noted that it was, in fact, covered. Still, Marcus Root, the photographer, never got back the $40,000 he invested in the Mount Vernon.[6]

Land Swaps and Railroad Tracks

The tract of land where the Mount Vernon Hotel apparently sat and the immediately adjacent land that became South Cape May were purchased by Mark Devine, an Irish immigrant who lived in Philadelphia, having arrived there in 1829 at the age of twenty-two. Devine owned a grocery

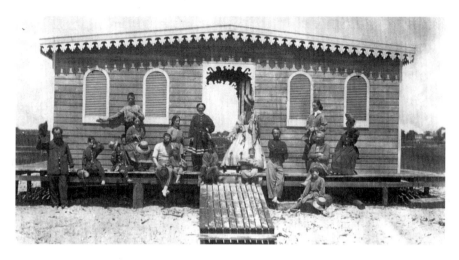

Mark Devine's private bathhouse at Cape May, 1865. *Courtesy of Don Pocher.*

store in Philadelphia and was a flour merchant, and he was also involved in a number of other endeavors. Philadelphia's Friendly Sons of St. Patrick credited him as the principal founder—the "originator"—of the Beneficial Saving Fund Society, obtaining its charter and purchasing the property in Philadelphia where it stood for its first 140 years. The society, which later became the Beneficial Savings Bank, was started in 1853 to aid the wave of Irish immigrants to Philadelphia during the potato famine. The bank still stands today, although its official history cites Philadelphia bishop John Neumann, canonized as a saint in 1977, as its inspirational catalyst. The Friendly Sons also credit Mark Devine with playing an important role in founding another major Philadelphia institution, St. Joseph's Hospital, established in the late 1840s, also principally to aid Irish immigrants. Aside from his work as a merchant and a community leader, Devine was an active investor in real estate in Philadelphia as well as in Cape May, where he made a series of purchases over time, dating back to 1839, beginning with a parcel of eighty-nine acres bought at a sheriff's sale.[7]

Devine didn't develop the land around South Cape May himself, but there was an important major improvement during the time he held it. Although the West Jersey Railroad offered rail service to Cape May starting in the 1860s, by the late 1870s and '80s, the *Republic*, a side-wheel steamboat, was still a major mode of transportation from Philadelphia to Cape May, landing at the Delaware Bay side of the Cape May peninsula near Cape May Point, almost three miles from the main settlement of Cape Island.

In 1879, Jonathan Cone, the owner of the *Republic*, developed the Delaware Bay and Cape May Railroad as a new means of transporting passengers from the steamboat, providing steam locomotive service and taking over the defunct Cape May and Sea Grove Horse-car Railroad. (Electric trolleys replaced the locomotives in 1892.) Cone improved the narrow-gauge rail tracks that went through Cape May Point—then called Sea Grove—past its landmark lighthouse and along the beach toward the West Jersey Railroad's Sea Breeze Excursion House in Cape May, right through the beachfront area owned by Mark Devine that became South Cape May.

A survey completed in 1886—a year after Devine's death—on file at the county clerk archives shows parts of the South Cape May area as still being in Devine's possession (or that of his estate). Contradicting this, though, is a news report in 1882 that Devine sold the land—the Mount Vernon Hotel tract being purchased by "a syndicate" and the land between that tract and Cape May Point (or what became South Cape May) purchased by Georgeanna Edmunds, wife of James Henry Edmunds.[8] The mayor of Cape May City in the 1880s and '90s, J. Henry Edmunds, was involved in a wide range of Cape May area enterprises, from water, gas and telephone companies to a steamboat, horse-racing park and the *Cape May Wave* newspaper.

The hotel tract was described as taking up two hundred acres, and the tract bought in Georgeanna Edmunds's name was described as larger and taking up 2,500 feet of beachfront. Other records appear to confirm that the land was out of Devine's hands by 1882—the Neptune Land Company was incorporated in that year to develop the former Devine property, with Theodore M. Reger, a leading principal of the company. Reger was another Philadelphian and served as secretary of the Franklin Fire Insurance Company there, in addition to making many investments in real estate in Philadelphia and Cape May, where he was involved in a number of development companies besides Neptune—the Rutherford Land Company, the West Cape May Improvement Company and the Mount Vernon Land Company among them.

The Elephant

The first structure built on the area that became South Cape May was an unusual one: a more than fifty-foot-tall building in the shape of an elephant, including a nearly twelve-foot-high observatory on the top taking the form of a howdah. At first dubbed "Light of Asia," the South Cape May building may have been named for the supposed albino elephant introduced in the United States by Adam Forepaugh, a competitor of circus masters P.T. Barnum and Ringling Brothers. Ultimately, though, the South Cape May elephant was known by locals as "Jumbo," after the highly publicized six-and-a-half-ton elephant the Barnum & Bailey Circus bought from the London Zoo in the early 1880s.[9] The original contract for constructing the building can be found at the Athenaeum of Philadelphia, thanks to one of the curators, who recovered it from a dumpster in Cape May, along with other records of early buildings in the area, including the earliest residences built in South Cape May.

Theodore Reger contracted with a builder, James Brady, to have the structure erected according to plans by Philadelphia architect Nathan H. Culver in April 1884. The cost was $18,000. Culver wasn't the first to design an elephant-shaped building. James V. Lafferty was responsible for two other similar structures: Lucy the Margate Elephant, outside of Atlantic City, built in 1881—still standing today—and Elephantine Colossus, in Coney Island, built in 1884. Lafferty held an American patent for an elephant-shaped building, but the idea dated back to French architect Charles-François Ribart, who planned one in 1758 to be constructed where the Arc de Triomphe now stands, although his plans went unrealized.

Jumbo originally stood near the beach toward the end of a road lane that ran toward the beach off Cape Island Turnpike, now called Sunset Boulevard, the main thoroughfare built in 1852 from Cape May City to the steamboat landing. That lane was later dubbed Sixteenth Avenue in South Cape May. Jumbo was positioned with its head toward the ocean, not far from the tracks of the Delaware Bay and Cape May Railroad, and trolley cars went by it every twenty minutes in the summer.

The elephant building was scheduled to be completed in July 1884, and Reger optimistically placed a newspaper ad in late June noting, "Parties wishing room in the Elephant to sell Soda Water, Fancy Articles, Advertising, Etc., and privileges for Bath Houses, Ice Cream Garden and Dairy should apply on the premises or to T.M. Reger, 508 Walnut Street, Philadelphia." But by October, work was still underway. Its "epidermis"—supplied by Philadelphia tinsmith Robert Givson—was spread out on a vacant lot near a church in Cape May City in October. By July 1885, it still hadn't been completed, although it was announced that it would be soon. Reger or a fellow promoter was probably the source of reports that the finished structure contained over one million pieces of wood, 250 kegs of nails, five tons of hardware and 13,400 square feet of tin.

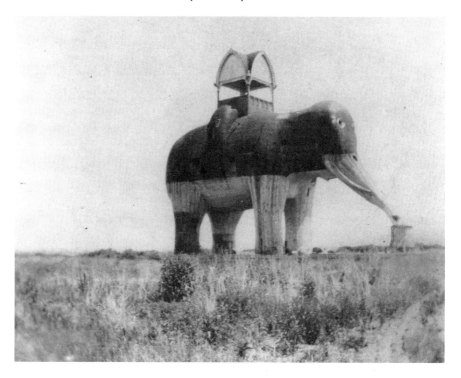

Light of Asia, elephant-shaped building constructed in 1885. *Courtesy of Cape May County Historical and Genealogical Society.*

The entrance into the body of the structure was in the hind legs, via a spiral staircase. The eyes were windows, and there were windows in various other parts of the body. There were stairs on both sides of the belly up to the howdah observatory, which treated visitors to expansive views of the ocean, bay and the Cape May area community. Tables and chairs were set up on the platform under Jumbo, where visitors enjoyed refreshments that were sold along with souvenirs at stands in the front legs. On at least one occasion, a church youth group camped out overnight on the platform.

Local historian John C. Alexander once recalled hearing long ago from an area resident who used to sneak inside of Jumbo as a boy with his friends to avoid paying the ten-cent admission fee. They crawled in through a loose board at the end of the trunk and climbed up through broken laths and plaster to a room at the elephant's head. Had Jumbo still been around when my brothers and I were in South Cape May, I'm sure we would have done the exact same thing, but the elephant was long gone by then. A victim of the weather and lack of upkeep, the elephant deteriorated over the years, its legs eventually falling through its wooden platform, and in the spring of 1900, it was demolished.

Still, Jumbo served a purpose for a time, and not only as an amusement for the locals. By 1887, the Neptune Land Company was out of the picture, and the Mount Vernon Land Company was the entity that owned the elephant and the surrounding land that became South Cape May. The company, which eventually sold some five hundred deeds to property in the area, used Jumbo as a billboard, painting "New Mount Vernon" on the elephant's side. That name was assigned to the new hotel built right near the elephant and, briefly, to the development overall, but the area was more widely known as the Mount Vernon tract or simply Mount Vernon until it was incorporated as the borough of South Cape May in 1894.

The old name was a carryover from the Mount Vernon House and Mount Vernon Hotel, and it's the source of some confusion, since "Mount Vernon tract" has also been used to describe the location of the former site of the Mount Vernon Hotel that was apparently near Broadway in Cape May City. There's plenty of irony in the name, too, if you think about it—there was nothing "mountainous" about this patch of land barely above sea level.

CHAPTER 2

The First Homes and
First Families of Mount Vernon
and South Cape May

THE FIRST ARCHITECTURAL GEMS

Three years after the novelty elephant building was finished, work to build
the community that became South Cape May started with a bang: a line of
several houses along the beach all designed by the most prominent architect
working in the Cape May area, Stephen Decatur Button. Relatively large,
two-and-a-half-story buildings with striking steeple-like front-corner towers
each topped by an observatory, the houses were prominently featured in
a twenty-four-page promotional brochure for "Mount Vernon Beach" put
together by the Mount Vernon Land Company.

The houses followed a design slightly resembling one of Button's most
renowned projects, but on a smaller scale—the residence commissioned for
John McCreary, a Philadelphia merchant. Now known as the Abbey and
operating as a bed-and-breakfast, the McCreary residence was built in the
winter of 1869–70. The McCreary residence was one of Button's most
elaborate houses and was especially notable for the departure the architect
took from his Italianate leanings into Gothic-influenced design.[10]

Although Button's work is described in a number of books and articles
on Cape May architecture, as of this writing, none appears to attribute
the South Cape May houses directly to him. The evidence that they
were designed by Button is clear, though. Work to build the first four of
the homes was covered by a single contract signed on April 10, 1888.

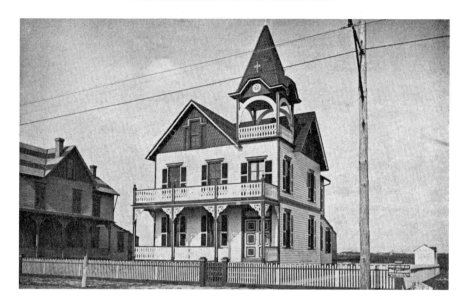

Home of the Lonabaugh family, circa 1892. *Courtesy of Cape May County Historical and Genealogical Society.*

They followed two basic building plans, with detailed specifications and drawings attributed to "S.D. Button, Archt. of No. 430 Walnut St. Philada. Pa." The four houses were to be built by the local Cape May construction firm of Cassedy and Hand for four of the principal officers of the Mount Vernon Land Company—although the company is not mentioned in the contract—John E. Lonabaugh, Eduard Buchholz, Edward Hagan and George Schwinn. (J. Henry Edmunds countersigned the contract.) The total cost of the four houses was $8,240. That contract was followed by another one for a single home built for another Mount Vernon officer, Peter Day, signed in June 1888. While the contracts' written specifications survive, the drawings do not. Still, the specifications provide detail about the building materials, including octagon- or diamond-shaped shingles on roofs and gables, and about the towers, observatories and "neat galvanized iron finials" on the observatory roofs, "painted French blue."[11]

Newspaper accounts in the spring and summer of 1888 give evidence that the houses were under construction or completed, although they don't mention Button. In March and April 1888, the *Star of the Cape* reported that John Lonabaugh visited the Cape May area to consult local carpenters about building houses on the Mount Vernon Land Company's tract, and in June, the paper reported that Peter Day had contracted to have his house

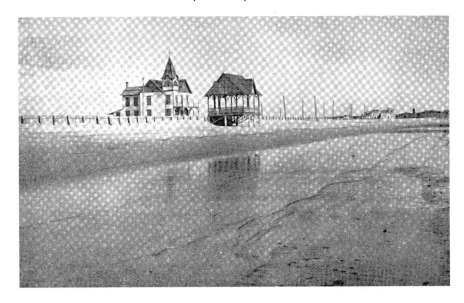

View from Eighth Avenue in Mount Vernon, circa 1892. *Courtesy of Cape May County Historical and Genealogical Society.*

built on the tract. In August 1888, the *Star of the Cape* devoted seven inches of news copy about the Mount Vernon tract, noting that eight houses were under construction, "several of which are now completed…and they are very ornamental in design." The article announced, "It will pay those who have not already done so to visit the Mount Vernon tract and take note of the improvements going on there. The energy being displayed in putting it in order for speedy settlement is one of the hopeful signs of the times for Cape May." Later that month, the newspaper noted that the Mount Vernon Association was constructing a substantial boardwalk fronting the properties along the beach, in hopes of connecting with the Cape May City boardwalk and Cape May Point to create a continuous promenade.[12]

Aside from the contracts and news accounts, there is some other less direct evidence—although visually dramatic—in the architect's personal library that the early South Cape May houses were designed by Button.[13] One of the books he consulted most heavily was James Fergusson's *The Illustrated Handbook of Architecture* (London, 1855). Included there—in a section describing examples of Gothic style in Italy—is an illustration that jumps out as surprisingly similar to Button's South Cape May houses: the north porch of the Church of Santa Maria Maggiore, a fourteenth-century addition to the twelfth-century church in Bergamo at the foothills of the Alps in northern Italy.[14]

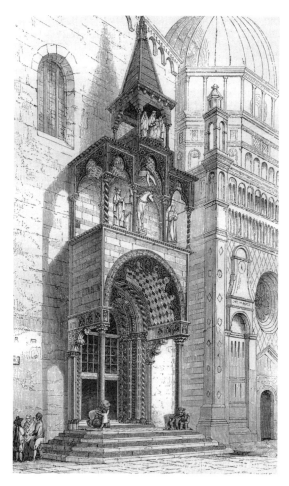

The north porch of the Church of St. Maria Maggiore, Italy. *James Fergusson*, The Illustrated Handbook of Architecture, *1855*.

Button's South Cape May houses were built toward the end of his career, when he was seventy-five years old, although he designed another notable series of Cape May–area homes three years later, in 1891, on Jackson Street in Cape May City, known as the Atlantic Terrace houses or the "Seven Sisters." His first commission in Cape May was in 1863, when John C. Bullitt hired him to make improvements on the Columbia Hotel. Bullitt was a major Cape May real estate developer and investor who had worked as a corporate lawyer for the Pennsylvania and Reading Railroads in Philadelphia at the same time that Button designed buildings for them. Born in Preston, Connecticut, in 1813 and named for Stephen Decatur, the War of 1812 hero who coincidentally summered in Cape May for years, Button worked in the building trades in New York and Hoboken as a young man and spent time in the South, where he won a competition to design the Alabama State Capitol in the 1840s. He moved to the Philadelphia area in 1848, first working in a partnership in the city with his brother-in-law, Joseph C. Hoxie. Button commuted from his home in Camden, New Jersey, where he once counted poet Walt Whitman among his neighbors. The partnership with Hoxie was short-lived; Button soon had his own architecture practice, carrying out several commissions for prominent clients, and he was a leading

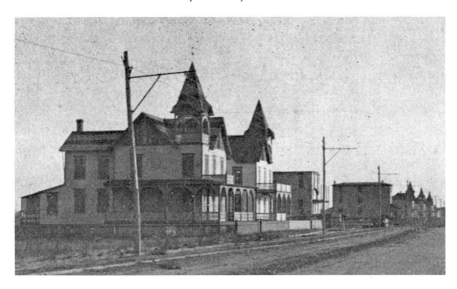

View from Thirteenth Avenue with the Day and Lonabaugh houses in forefront, circa 1892. *Courtesy of Cape May County Historical and Genealogical Society.*

Philadelphia architect at the height of his career when he began working on projects in Cape May. Notable designs of his include the Stockton Hotel, the Sea Breeze Excursion House and the Windsor and Lafayette Hotels, along with the Jackson Clubhouse (a private gambling house that's now the Mainstay, a popular bed-and-breakfast) and many residences—possibly totaling nearly fifty buildings altogether, including the ones designed for the Mount Vernon tract that became South Cape May.

In all, there appear to have been as many as nine houses built on the tract using Button's corner-tower design, evidenced by the house-footprint diagrams included in the 1890 *Insurance Maps of the New Jersey Coast* published by the Sanborn-Perris Map Company. Cape May City Hall holds a hand-annotated version of the portion of that set containing Cape May maps—marked as being updated through 1902—that is especially notable, since it indicates the names of the houses' owners. There was probably at least one more house designed by Button in the development, as well, as apparent from the surviving building contract for a two-story house with a mansard roof in the Mount Vernon tract for Philadelphia cutlery merchant Charles R. Windhoeval.

THE FAMILIES IN THE HOMES DESIGNED BY BUTTON

Remarkably, four of those corner-tower houses of Button's still stand today. Like several other homes in the borough, they were moved from their beachfront locations early in the twentieth century to their present sites in Cape May City, near the original location of the Mount Vernon Hotel. In those days, the wholesale, physical move of an entire house was a relatively common occurrence in the Cape May area, sometimes involving a simple move of a hundred feet or more from the shoreline and sometimes a move to another location a mile or more away. Local contractors would advertise house-moving services widely, as Samuel E. Ewing did on the front page of the *Star of the Cape* on October 30, 1897, after one of the biggest nor'easters in years. Three of the four surviving houses designed by Button were moved in the first few years of the twentieth century, possibly in 1903. The annotated Sanborn-Perris map dated 1902 notes that three were moved, but the moves may actually have taken place later. At least one of the other South Cape May homes noted on the map—owned by Theodophilus Fenn—was actually moved in 1903. The *Star of the Cape* reported that several homes were relocated after a severe mid-October storm and described three houses in the borough as being "washed down"—completely destroyed or nearly so.[15]

Like Windhoeval, Mark Devine, Theodore Reger and many other figures in Cape May's early history, the owners of the corner-tower houses designed by Button were mainly Philadelphians, and they, too, were largely involved with the overall development of the Mount Vernon tract.

John Lonabaugh, who had the lead name on the contract to build the first four houses, was a Civil War veteran who had a printing business and was active in the Order of Cadets of Temperance in Philadelphia, serving as grand marshal of its annual parade in 1873. He and his wife, Margaret, had three children: Ella, Maggie and John Jr., their youngest, born in 1888, the year their house on the beach was built.[16] The elder Lonabaugh took a leading role in the incorporation of the Mount Vernon community as its own municipality under the name of South Cape May. In records filed in the county clerk's office August 27, 1894, he's noted as swearing on behalf of petitioners who called for a special election to vote on the borough's incorporation—with Lonabaugh serving as an election clerk. The borough was, essentially, seceding from the borough of West Cape May, which had been formed in 1884 from parts of Lower Township. Lonabaugh did not live long to enjoy his summer house, though; he died in 1896. His house,

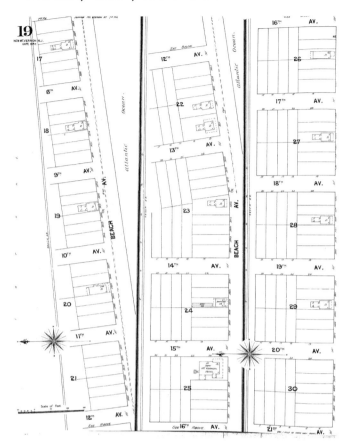

New Mount Vernon, New Jersey (Cape May). Sanborn-Perris map, 1890. *Used with permission from the Sanborn Library, LLC. Obtained from the* ProQuest Digital Sanborn Maps® 1867–1970 *online database.*

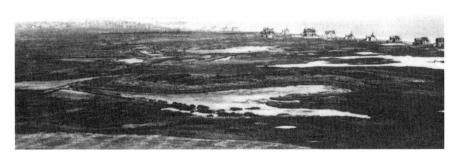

View from Cape May Point Lighthouse, postcard circa 1892. *Courtesy of Robert W. Elwell Sr.*

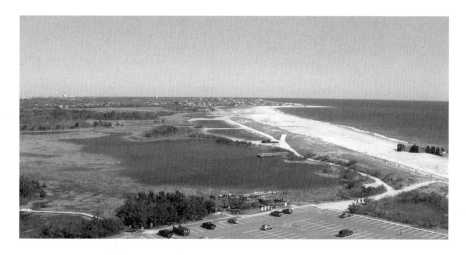

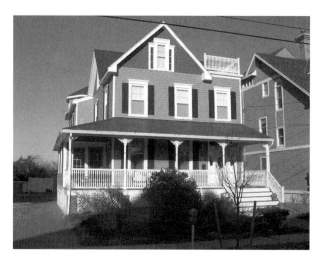

Above: View of South Cape May Meadows, 2010. *Photo by Robert Kenselaar.*

Left: Former home of the Lonabaugh family (minus corner tower roof) now at 16 Second Avenue. *Photo by Robert Kenselaar.*

originally situated on Beach Avenue between Twelfth and Thirteenth Avenues, was featured and identified in the Mount Vernon Beach brochure printed about 1892. According to the annotated Sanborn-Perris map in Cape May City Hall, the house was moved to Second Avenue in Cape May City. The house now at 16 Second Avenue appears to be the former Lonabaugh home, although the top-tower observatory and roof are now gone and a large addition was built onto the back of the house in recent years.[17]

Other notable owners of the Button-designed Mount Vernon tract homes included Peter Day, George Rutherford, Eduard Buchholz and Samuel Bailie. Day was a well-known Philadelphia manufacturer who founded the firm of

Day & Frick, producing the widely popular Day's Soap, and he and his wife had a large family of six children. The Days' home was also prominently featured in the Mount Vernon Beach brochure. It was originally situated at the corner of Thirteenth Avenue next to the Lonabaughs' on Beach Avenue. In its original location in line with the others, the tracks for the trolley that ran between Cape May City and Cape May Point were located behind the house, but sometime in the first couple of years of the twentieth century it was moved behind those tracks and probably closer east toward the C'ape May City line. The Day house does not appear to have survived.

George Rutherford is identified on the Cape May City Hall Sanborn-Perris map as the owner of the corner-tower Button house originally located the farthest east in Mount Vernon or South Cape May, between Seventh and Eighth Avenues. Members of the Rutherford family were longtime residents of the Cape May area, and they owned a seven-acre farm within the borough of South Cape May. The Sanborn-Perris map indicates that George Rutherford's home was moved to Cape May City, and subsequent owners of the house, at 10 South Broadway, included Gideon Stull and, later, Anne Pratt. Anne remembers an old-timer in the neighborhood telling her about seeing South Cape May houses moved to Broadway, laid over on their sides on trolley tracks and pulled by mules.

In addition to Lonabaugh, another of the original Button-designed house owners who was also very active in the community was Eduard Buchholz, who served as president of the Mount Vernon Land

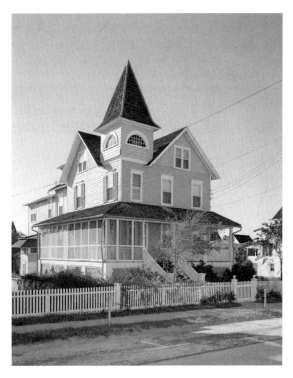

Former Rutherford family home, now at 10 South Broadway. *Library of Congress, Historic American Buildings Survey, HABS NJ-574.*

Company and the South Cape May Cottagers' Association. Like several other early residents, Buchholz was a German American who lived in the Germantown section of Philadelphia. (A group of 150 German Americans made an excursion from Philadelphia to Cape May in 1892, with several investigating Mount Vernon tract lots.) Buchholz is mentioned a good deal in the gossipy news snippets about Mount Vernon and South Cape May that appeared in the *Star of the Cape* newspaper in the 1890s, and he and his family are credited with organizing a number of social activities, including fishing trips, watermelon parties and a hay ride. His name appeared in the Philadelphia newspapers in later years as well (variously as "Eduard" and "Edward"), as he became deeply involved in Philadelphia city government through the 1920s, serving as common councilman, select councilman of the Nineteenth Ward, chairman of the school committee and a spokesman for German American Republicans who campaigned strongly for Theodore Roosevelt's U.S. presidential run.[18]

Shortly after 1900, the former Buchholz family home was purchased by another family prominent in both Philadelphia and the Cape May area, the Wilbrahams. John W. Wilbraham, a leader in the Philadelphia-area iron industry, purchased the house about the same time that he bought a property

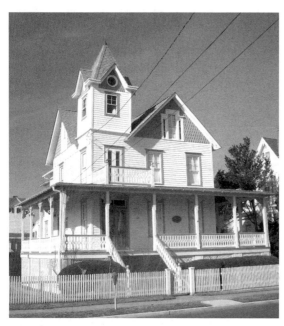

Former Buchholz and Wilbraham family home, now at 18 First Avenue. *Photo by Robert Kenselaar.*

on what is now Myrtle Avenue in West Cape May, which included a simple farmhouse that he expanded considerably. He had train tracks built on that West Cape May property for his own direct railroad car service, leading right to the northwest side entrance of the house. Wilbraham was a generous philanthropist in the Cape May area, donating property that became Wilbraham Park in West Cape May, and his former house in that borough still exists, now as a bed-and-breakfast known as the Wilbraham Mansion. He made a major change to his South Cape May house also, which would have been unusual almost anywhere else. Like others in the community, he had his house moved, joining other former South Cape May homes that relocated to the same area of Cape May City. At its 18 First Avenue location, the house stayed in the Wilbraham family up until the late 1990s, when present owners Jim and Gloria Edwards purchased it and carried out extensive restoration work on it. (Jim notes that etched into the tower of his house are the names of two other South Cape May residents, Helen Hartranft and Howard Hay, with a date, August 1898.)

The fourth remaining South Cape May house designed by Stephen Decatur Button has stayed in the same family from the time it was built. Originally owned by Samuel Bailie, a grocer and wholesale sugar merchant in Philadelphia, the house remained in South Cape May longer than the others—until about 1918—eventually moving to 12 South Broadway, right next door to the Rutherford house, which had been moved about fifteen years earlier. Bailie and his wife, Annabella, had five children, and according to Don Foster, one of their great-grandchildren, family legend had it that the house was built for their only daughter, his grandmother Agnes, shortly after she was born. The Bailie house was originally situated between Thirteenth and Fourteenth Avenues, on a spot where there was a slight bend in the shoreline in South Cape May. As Eleanor Graham Foster, Bailie's granddaughter, noted in an article in the *Cape May Star and Wave* of July 4, 1985, Bailie tried to protect his South Cape May home by having a bulkhead

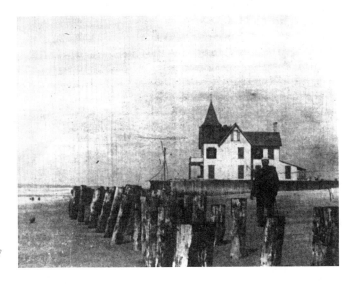

Bailie home in South Cape May, circa 1910s. *Courtesy of Tom Dvorschak.*

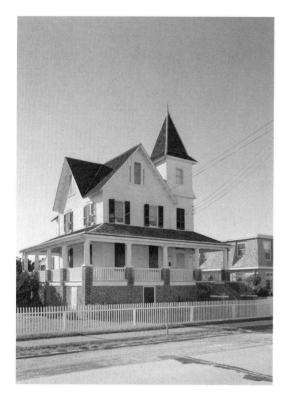

Former home of Samuel Bailie, now at 12 South Broadway, as photographed in 1977. *Library of Congress, Historic American Buildings Survey, HABS NJ-575.*

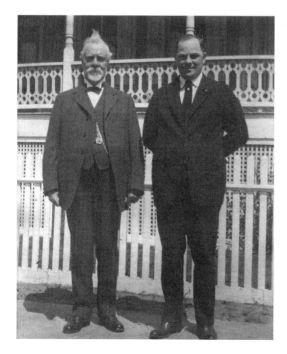

Samuel Bailie Sr. and his son, Samuel Jr., outside the son's home at 9 South Broadway, circa 1920s. *Courtesy of Don Foster.*

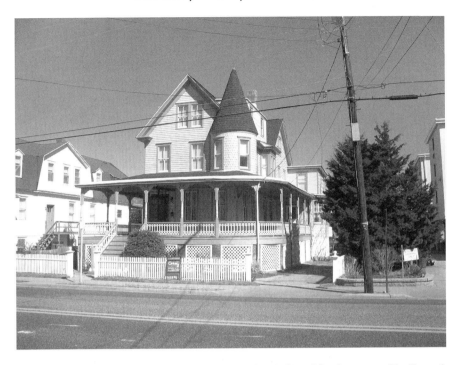

Former home of Theodophilus Fenn, originally in South Cape May, later owned by Samuel Bailie Jr., now at 9 South Broadway. *Photo by Robert Kenselaar.*

built around it after the other homes alongside it were gone and after shifts in the shoreline accelerated with the 1913 construction of the major jetty at Cape May Inlet by the Army Corps of Engineers. During the winter of 1917–18—one of the coldest on record at the time—the porch of the house was washed away, and Bailie soon decided to move the house, as Mrs. Foster reported, accomplished by workmen using oxen and huge wooden rollers. Bailie's son, Samuel Bailie Jr., later purchased another house that was originally located in South Cape May—the home owned by Theodophilus Fenn, which was moved to 19 South Broadway, across the street from the elder Bailie's home.[19]

CHAPTER 3

More Houses, Families and a Hotel

A New-Style Hotel and More Homes by Another Noted Architect

In addition to Stephen Decatur Button, another prominent architect designed homes in South Cape May: Enos R. Williams. Unlike Button, Williams was not a member of the elite architectural circles of Philadelphia; he was a Cape May local, having moved there from his birthplace in Atlantic County, New Jersey, after serving in the military during the Civil War. He earned a solid reputation as a builder and contractor and eventually developed considerable skill as an architect. He also became involved in local politics, serving on the Cape May City Council and making a run for the state legislature. Architectural historians George E. Thomas and Carl E. Doebley credit Williams with generating the last wave of stylistic changes in Cape May architecture, calling him "the most interesting architect in the community" during the 1880s and 1890s.[20] Williams was actually called upon to design houses in the area that became South Cape May before Button. In early 1884, plans were in the works for a contractor to build twenty-five houses designed by Williams on the Neptune Land Company's tract,[21] but this work apparently didn't take place. There's no mention of these houses in the local newspapers during that year or the following one, and the first report of any residential construction is the work for John Lonabaugh and others in 1888. The 1890 Sanborn-Perris map for the Mount Vernon tract shows only thirteen buildings.

In Mount Vernon, Williams was responsible for designing its major hotel, built in 1889, a year after the first Button-designed residences.[22] At first known as the New Mount Vernon Hotel and later as the Cayman Hotel and South Cape May Hotel, the building is an example of the "shingle style" that Thomas and Doebley credit Williams with introducing to the Cape May area. The style is characterized by its simplicity and lack of ornamentation—and continuous wooden-shingle siding—and had arisen elsewhere in the northeast United States as early as the 1870s, running counter to earlier Victorian-era highly ornamented styles. Williams was responsible for the design of the hotel but not for building it. That task fell to Alexander Douglass, a contractor based in Philadelphia who did a considerable amount of work in Mount Vernon, living with his family in the New Mount Vernon Hotel during the off-season in 1890, for example, in order to work throughout the winter on building more homes in the borough. According to Eleanor Graham Foster, Douglass was brought in for work in South Cape May by Samuel Bailie, who was a cousin of Douglass's, and Bailie was among the officers of the Mount Vernon Improvement Company who signed the building contract for the hotel. Originally located at Beach and Fifteenth Avenues, the New Mount Vernon Hotel was moved back

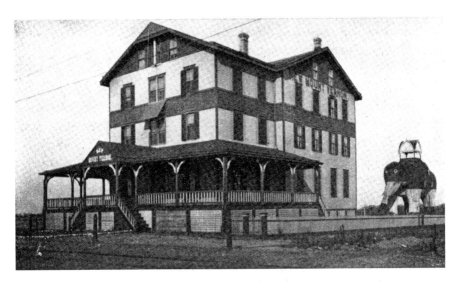

New Mount Vernon Hotel and Light of Asia. *Mount Vernon Beach* brochure. *Courtesy of Robert W. Elwell Sr.*

behind the trolley tracks and east to Eleventh Avenue shortly after 1900, where it remained standing through the 1930s.

In addition to the New Mount Vernon Hotel, there were a few other nonresidential buildings in South Cape May's early days—builders unknown—including bathhouses near the New Mount Vernon Hotel, owned by Charles Windhoeval; a sizable boardinghouse, Gabel's Beach Villa; the Union Auditorium, which held meetings and Sunday church services; a small borough hall; and a small beach pavilion near the shoreline.

Enos Williams was also responsible for designing residences for South Cape May families, one notable example being that of Francis S. and Adeline Rutschman. Francis S. Rutschman—also known as Frank—was South

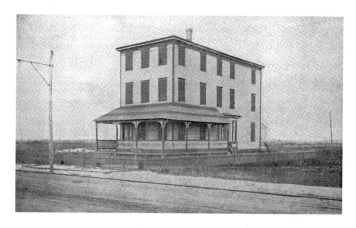

Gabel's Beach Villa, Beach and Tenth Avenues, circa 1892. *Courtesy of Cape May County Historical and Genealogical Society.*

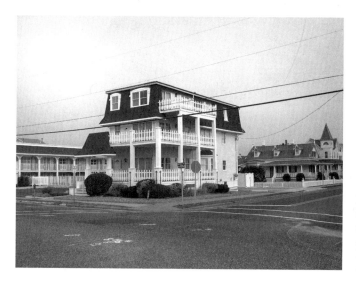

Former Gabel's Beach Villa, now at Beach Avenue and South Broadway. *Photo by Robert Kenselaar.*

Cape May's mayor from 1905 until his death in 1920; he was the second to hold the office, after James Ritchie Jr., and the longest-standing mayor of the borough. Rutschman was yet another Philadelphian, a manufacturer who made machinery to produce and process soap—such as Rutschman's Automatic Soap Chipper—so he and fellow South Cape May resident Peter Day had much in common. Adeline Rutschman was also active in the South Cape May community, hosting card-game parties on their porch, among other things, the game of choice being euchre. Adeline's father, Jacob Greenewald, and her sisters and brothers made visits to the Rutschmans' South Cape May home from time to time, her sister Jennie bringing her "wheel"—late nineteenth-century shorthand for bicycle. Frank and Adeline's son, Elwood Charles Rutschman, was in his mid-teens when the family's summer home was built, and he went on to become an accomplished athlete who helped establish the intercollegiate basketball team at the University of Pennsylvania in 1903. Known as "Rutsch," Elwood ran cross-country for Penn, won tournaments at the Cape May Golf Club, reported about sports in newspapers and was a referee for the first American pro basketball league. He died young, of tuberculosis, in 1911 at age thirty-four.

Built in 1892 by the contractors Church and Elwell according to Enos Williams's design, the Rutschman house was part of a second wave of

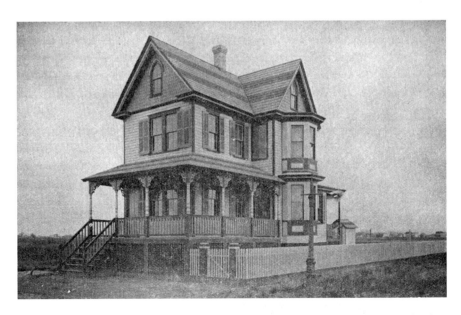

Rutschman house on Eighth Avenue, circa 1892. *Courtesy of Cape May County Historical and Genealogical Society.*

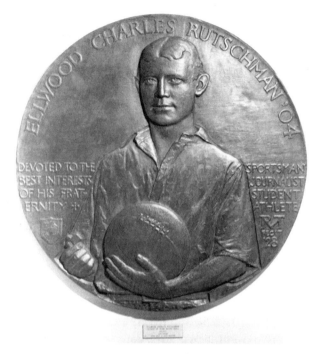

Plaque honoring Elwood C. Rutschman, a founder of the University of Pennsylvania's basketball program. *University of Pennsylvania Archives.*

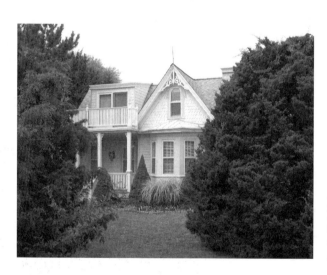

Former Rutschman house, now at 601 Sunset Boulevard, West Cape May. *Photo by Robert Kenselaar.*

building, not situated on the beachfront but about a block away, on Eighth Avenue. The house was not markedly stylized like the New Mount Vernon Hotel but was in keeping with the relatively simple, peaked-roof homes in the area at the time, including a porch with Victorian spandrel ornamentation (or gingerbread) and featuring a two-story bay-window section. The house was another survivor, but it was moved much later, in the mid-1950s, to a different location than where others were moved—to Sunset Boulevard at the corner of Bayshore Road in West Cape May. Sunset Boulevard is where two Burcher family homes were moved from South Cape May about the same time, and the former Rutschman home is two houses away from where I built my own cottage on Sunset Boulevard in 1952. Painted pink in recent years, the house has a hand-painted sign on the property dubbing it the "Seaworthy Angel." Actually, only a portion of the house was moved—its second and third floors. The first floor was badly damaged in storms over the years.

Other houses built a block or more behind the beachfront in South Cape May resembled the Rutschmans', and at least one, a house built for John P. Miller and his family, was based on the same design by Williams. Miller owned a men's clothing store on South Eighth Street in Philadelphia, and his family immigrated to the United States from Munich, Germany, when he and his brother Jacob were young, just before the Civil War. They were orphaned shortly after their family arrived and were drafted into the

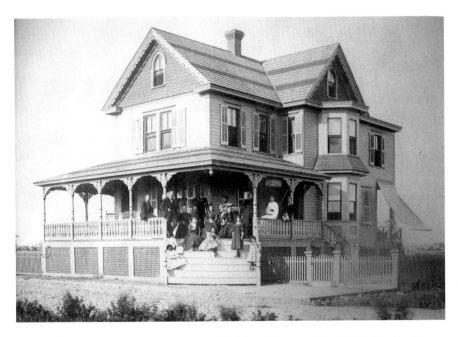

John P. Miller and family on Ninth Avenue in Mount Vernon, circa 1893. *Courtesy of Miriam Pedrick.*

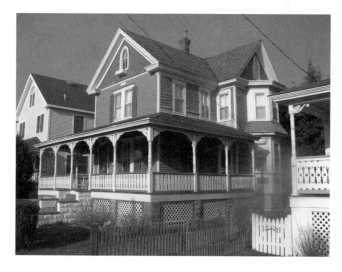

Former home of John P. Miller family, now at 37 First Avenue. *Photo by Robert Kenselaar.*

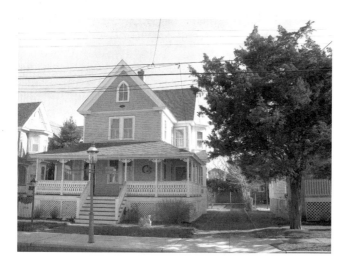

Former South Cape May house, also owned by members of the Miller family, now at 35 First Avenue. *Photo by Robert Kenselaar.*

Union army, with John finishing his tour of duty as a sergeant, fighting at Gettysburg and getting wounded at the Battle of Spotsylvania Court House in 1864.

Church and Elwell were the builders of John Miller's Mount Vernon tract home, and the building contract noted that the house was to be constructed according to the same plan as the Rutschmans', adding one bedroom. The house was completed in July 1893, when the *Star of the Cape* reported jokingly that John Miller was "fairly domiciled in his new cottage on Ninth Avenue.

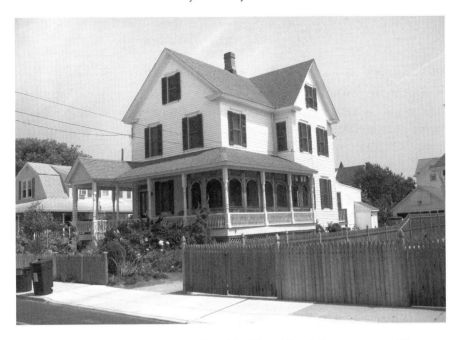

Former South Cape May house, originally at Twelfth and Beach Avenues, now at 21 Second Avenue. *Photo by Robert Kenselaar.*

His family is composed of himself and wife, and nine children, a sister-in-law and a servant, making thirteen persons, yet he does not consider himself an unlucky man." The house was ultimately moved to the neighborhood in Cape May City where other South Cape May homes were moved, to First Avenue. Interestingly, the property next to John Miller's on that street was partly owned by his brother, Jacob, along with members of the Herzberg family, who together purchased it from Elizabeth L. Devine, Mark Devine's widow, in 1891. Jacob Miller and the Herzbergs were members of the Congregation Rodeph Shalom, Philadelphia's historic synagogue founded in 1795, as was Jacob Greenewald, Adeline Rutschman's father, and others in the Greenewald family. According to Miriam Pedrick, the current owner of the former Jacob Miller property, her house was also originally in South Cape May and also in the Miller family. Some years ago, she and her neighbor got a delightful surprise when John Miller's great-grandson, Andrew Finlayson, showed up one day and dropped off beautifully framed copies of a vintage picture of his great-grandfather's house at its original South Cape May location along with information about the family's history in the borough.[23]

OTHER EARLY HOUSES

Other notable examples of South Cape May architecture—although their designers are unknown—include the Queen Anne–style home owned by Theodophilus Fenn now located on South Broadway and the Stick-style home built in 1892 and owned by William F. Borzell, which didn't survive but was featured in the Mount Vernon Beach brochure. Although Borzell was the owner, the first residents of his Eighth Avenue house were renters: the family of South Cape May's first mayor, James Ritchie Jr.[24]

The home of the family of Charles G. Marshall, a Philadelphia foundryman, was another house featured in the brochure, shown in a photograph with its neighbor, the Rutschman house. The *Star of the Cape* provides a good record of the Marshall home's progress: Samuel Ewing, who had recently finished grading and laying out Seventh Avenue for the first time, set the foundation in February 1891. Contractors were finished in time for the Marshalls to occupy the house by Easter. The owners were "highly pleased with it, particularly with the artistic skill of Messrs. Schillinger & Woolson in tinting the white coat of plaster." The Marshall and Fenn homes were mentioned in particular in 1903 when a group of South Cape May homes were moved to the western end of Cape May City, the Marshall home to First Avenue and the Fenn home to South Broadway.[25]

One final house I'll mention in detail has, like Samuel Bailie's house, remained in the same family since the day it was built: the home of Thomas H. Weinmann. Another Philadelphian, Weinmann was in the fabric-dying business, operating Thomas Weinmann & Sons on North Howard Street. His family's house in South Cape May was moved twice—it was originally set at Beach and Sixteenth Avenues, in line with the homes designed

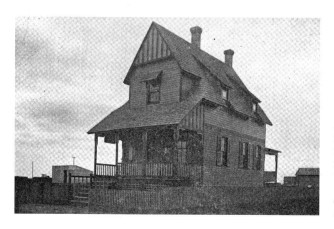

House of the William F. Borzell family on Eighth Avenue above Beach Avenue, circa 1892. *Courtesy of Cape May County Historical and Genealogical Society.*

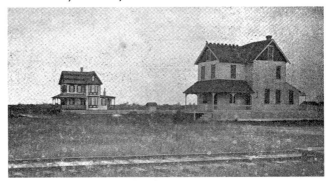

Homes of the Rutschman (left) and Marshall families (right) on Eighth Avenue, circa 1892. *Courtesy of Cape May County Historical and Genealogical Society.*

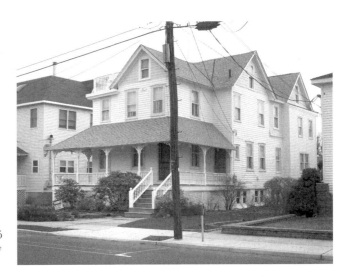

Former home of Charles G. Marshall and family, now at 25 First Avenue. *Photo by Robert Kenselaar.*

by Stephen Decatur Button, and was moved to Ninth Avenue in South Cape May in 1903 behind the trolley tracks,[26] next to the house owned by Thomas D. Caswell and his family—which my family would purchase later, in the 1920s. The Weinmann house was later moved to its final location, where it still stands today, at 15 First Avenue. Tom Dvorschak, a former nearby neighbor who has researched the history of local houses extensively, has seen one account noting that the Weinmann house was moved in 1918, about the same time as the Bailies'. Lee Krumenacker, Thomas Weinmann's great-granddaughter, remembers her grandmother telling her that the house movers put a glass of water on the dining room table before the move to prove that they would not spill one drop of water in the process of relocating the house—and supposedly, not one drop spilled. According to Lee, the home is recognized as a "key historic house"

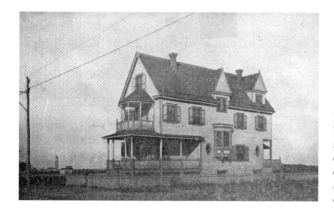

Home of Thomas Weinmann on Sixteenth and Beach Avenues, circa 1892. *Courtesy of Cape May County Historical and Genealogical Society.*

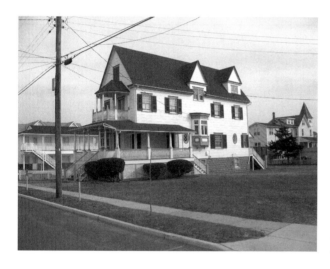

Former Weinmann house now at 15 First Avenue. *Photo by Robert Kenselaar.*

by Cape May City because of its architectural significance, with features such as its front second-floor bay porch area and third-floor wall dormers characteristic of Stick-style architecture.

LATER HOUSES

The major building boom in the community appears to have extended only into the mid-1890s. Another development nearly surfaced in the early 1910s, not in South Cape May but on a sliver of land just west of the borough, which Philadelphia lawyer J. Howard Weatherby attempted to market to the African American community but failed. One other real estate development in South Cape May succeeded in bringing in new life to the borough later on: a series of seven buildings holding twenty apartments altogether, known as the Spanish Villas. Set between Thirteenth and Fourteenth Avenues on Mount Vernon Avenue, the Spanish Villas were built in 1926 by the contracting firm Smedley Co. They included three larger buildings holding four apartments each and four smaller ones with two apartments each, with individual apartments a little less than one thousand square feet each. Blueprints of the overall development are in the county clerk's archives, showing garages in each of the buildings and concrete sidewalks all around. (Some accounts note that there were eight buildings in the Villas, but the blueprints show only seven.) The Spanish Villas had stucco exteriors, their design fitting in with the Spanish Revival style that was popular at the time and reflected in some other Cape May area buildings, such as the Cape Island Baptist Church built in 1916 at Columbia Avenue and Gurney Street in Cape May City. Original owners of the apartments included Frank Bowne and the Rutherford family, and later—by 1926—Margaret and Joseph Aylsworth, whose great-granddaughter, Courtney Romberger, still lives in the Cape May area. From what she's heard of her great-grandmother, Courtney thinks it's likely that Margaret Aylsworth designed and sewed the stylish outfit she's wearing in the photo of her at the entrance of one of the Villas. Another later owner was Ralph T. Stevens, who purchased four or five of the units. Stevens's son, Ralph Jr., recalls working there in the early 1940s when he was in his early teens, cleaning the units and helping with renting them out. One of the Spanish Villas survives today, relocated to 19 First Avenue in Cape May City.

Another building constructed after the first wave of development was the residence of David L. Kean, built in the bungalow style identified with the arts and crafts movement in the early twentieth century. The Kean house was located on the same lot in South Cape May where John P. Miller's house was originally located—on Ninth Avenue near the corner of Mount Vernon—before the Miller house was moved to First Avenue. Kean served as the tax collector and treasurer for South Cape May from 1927 to 1940, so he was on the borough's council with all the mayors in the 1920s and '30s except for Isaac Days, who was mayor for the first five years after Frank Rutschman died. The other mayors were James Cunningham, 1925 to 1933; Harvey Mentzer, 1933 to 1936 or '37; and Joseph W. Leahy, serving through 1940. (The last mayor, serving through 1945, was Willard P. Errickson, whom my father served with as borough clerk.)[27] Like my family, the Kean family was among the last residents of South Cape May. David L. Kean is the only

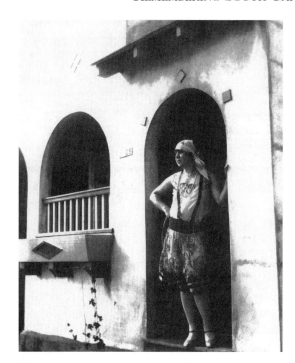

Left: Margaret Aylsworth at the Spanish Villas, circa 1926. *Courtesy of Courtney Romberger.*

Below: Spanish Villas in South Cape May, circa 1926. *Courtesy of Courtney Romberger.*

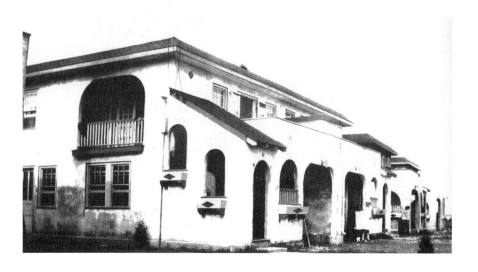

South Cape May resident listed in the Cape May phonebook from 1948 through 1950—my family did not have a phone there then—with Kean's address given as Ninth and Mount Vernon Avenues in the borough. In 1955, the phone directory lists him with the same phone number at 22 Broadway

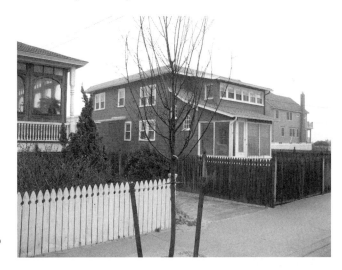

Surviving Spanish Villa, now at 19 Second Avenue. *Photo by Robert Kenselaar.*

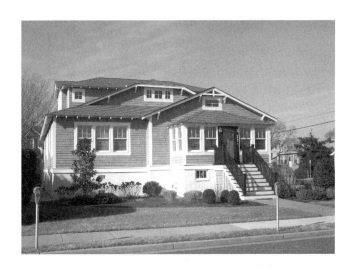

Former home of the Kean family, originally at Ninth and Mount Vernon Avenues in South Cape May, now at 22 South Broadway. *Photo by Robert Kenselaar.*

in Cape May City, where his house had been moved. His family's former home still stands today, beautifully restored and expanded.

Immediately next door to the former home of the Keans on Broadway is another former South Cape May house, also in the bungalow style, which was owned by our family's next-door neighbors on Ninth Avenue in the borough, the Watsons. Like the Keans' house, the Watsons' home was also originally built on a lot in South Cape May that was the site of another home that was moved to First Avenue in the early twentieth century—the one that belonged to Thomas Weinmann and his family. Unlike the other South

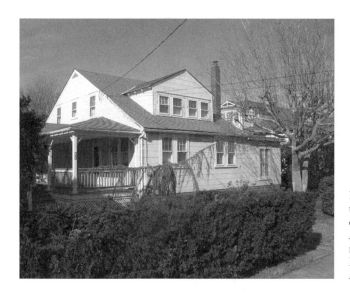

Former home of the Watson family, originally at Ninth Avenue beachfront, now at 20 South Broadway. *Photo by Robert Kenselaar.*

Cape May homes that were relocated, the Watsons' house wasn't moved wholesale, in one piece. Theirs was moved bit by bit, reconstructed after it was badly damaged by storms in the 1940s, as recalled by the Watsons' neighbor on Broadway, Eleanor Graham Foster, and Cliff Pearson, the current owner, who purchased the house from the Watsons.

BUILDING THE ROADS AND INFRASTRUCTURE

The Sanborn-Perris and Sanborn insurance maps are invaluable sources for studying the development of the South Cape May houses and their later relocations. The earliest maps of the borough show a lot of ambition on the part of its developers, dividing the area on paper into a detailed grid pattern of streets and avenues, with many plots of land. But, as aerial photographs of the area dating back to 1920 show, the detailed street grid planned by the developers wasn't really fully developed, and a number of streets initially laid out weren't kept over time. The streets that were fully developed and kept up over the years included Mount Vernon, Seventh, Eighth, Ninth and Twelfth Avenues.

In addition to the maps, the property deeds and tax records in the county clerk's archives and the surviving building contracts, other notable primary source materials documenting South Cape May's history include two sets of documents held at the New Jersey State Archives: the *Borough Council Minutes*, covering 1903 through 1935, and the *Ordinance Book* of 1911

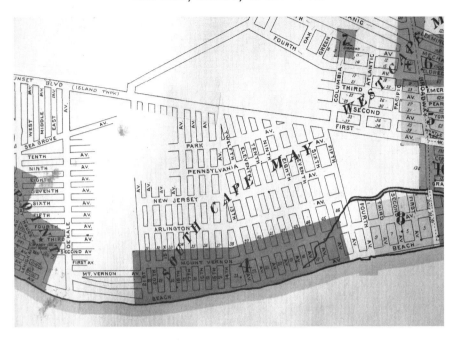

From the 1909 Sanborn map showing originally planned South Cape May streets. *Used with permission from the Sanborn Library, LLC.*

to 1918, both written in longhand. There's a good chance my father had these in his possession when he was borough clerk, and it would have been his responsibility to keep the minutes of the council as clerk, although the minutes from his years in that capacity, from 1941 to 1945, haven't survived.

The work involved in bringing electricity and phone service to the borough is described in considerable detail in the earlier minutes, along with problems with sanitation and various residents' delinquent tax payments. As noted in the minutes, the Cape May Light and Power Company started putting electricity in the borough in 1903. The borough council passed an ordinance granting the company "the right and privilege of erecting poles and stringing wires thereon." At the start, though, electricity was available only from 8:00 p.m. to midnight from the months of June through September. By 1911, the Delaware and Atlantic Telegraph and Telephone Company had begun to set phone and telegraph wiring in place. In 1916, the borough passed a health ordinance outlawing cesspools and protecting Cape Island Creek, which was used for household water. The ordinance required toilet facilities—"privies"—to be constructed to promote a healthy environment. The ordinances and borough minutes leave very little record of aspects of

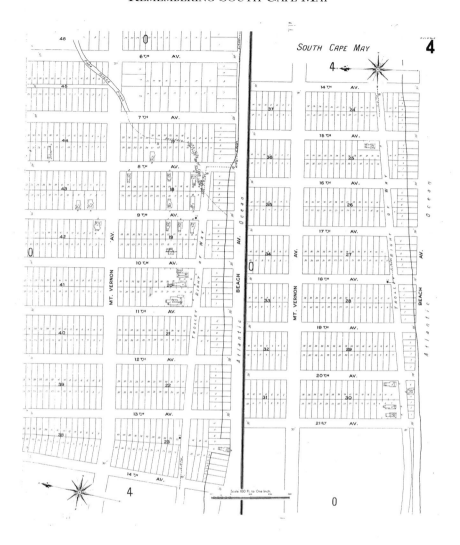

The 1909 Sanborn map, South Cape May. *Used with permission from the Sanborn Library, LLC. Obtained from the* ProQuest Digital Sanborn Maps® 1867–1970 *online database.*

life in South Cape May beyond the nuts and bolts of basic infrastructure, bills paid and taxes owed. Newspaper accounts do include some lively description of Mount Vernon and South Cape May social life, along with the storms that hit the community from its early days, as covered in the next chapter.

Total Housing Stock and Total Population

It's hard to say precisely how many homes were built in South Cape May or how many residents it had. There doesn't appear to be any surviving separate borough directory of names and addresses or any full, simple listing of the houses built in the borough. The borough council minutes mention dozens and dozens of residents' names, but not in an organized way, except occasionally in noting delinquent taxpayers. At the height of the summer season in 1892, the *Star of the Cape* announced that there were 284 people residing in Mount Vernon, including 98 guests at the New Mount Vernon Hotel, which was filled to capacity.[28] The petition filed to incorporate the borough in 1894 stated that the area took up two square miles and had a population of not fewer than 200 residing there for at least part of the year. But the New Jersey State Census in 1895 had the population count at 66, with fourteen households living in the same number of dwellings. In 1897, South Cape May's property assessment had been reduced from just over $100,000 to less than $55,000. You might think that meant that half the housing stock was moved, but it wasn't until 1903 that news reports described houses being moved to the west end of Cape May City, after the storms of that year. The U.S. Census in 1900 (taken in May) had the population at 14. The New Jersey State Census returns in 1905 showed only 6 residents in South Cape May but listed twenty-three "dwelling houses."[29] The county clerk's archives lists hundreds of property deeds sold by the Mount Vernon Land Company between 1888 and 1905—multiple deeds to several names—but this just confirms that plots of land were sold, not that houses were built on them.

The best estimate of the number of houses in South Cape May comes from the Sanborn maps compiled over the years and the aerial photos taken by the U.S. Army. Taking a close look at those, it appears that there were fewer than fifty buildings altogether in South Cape May. The highest count I come to is forty-two from the Sanborn map of 1929, found in the New Jersey State Library.

The Mount Vernon community and the borough of South Cape May seemed to show a lot of potential at the outset: its first homes and a sizable hotel were designed by leading architects in the area, and wealthy Philadelphia families settled in—the households of leading merchants and manufacturers from the city. But by the time my grandparents bought their property in the community in 1923, South Cape May was just a modest little beach community.

CHAPTER 4

Vacation Living, Storms and a Ghost

LIFE ON THE BEACH

Some of the early notices in local newspapers about Mount Vernon and South Cape May sounded a lot like real estate press releases: "Whew! What an airy place is the namesake of the famous country seat of the Father of his country. Sea breezes all the time and each cottage with enough ground around it to permit the full sweep of the wind. And how the people enjoy it and thrive, too on the keen, bracing color-giving air which is such an attraction at this place."[30]

In the early years especially, the *Star of the Cape* regularly covered local news in small sections—usually twenty lines or so—under the headings "Mount Vernon" and, later, "South Cape May," on pages devoted to various communities near Cape May City such as West Cape May and Cape May Point. (Before the two newspapers merged in 1907, the competing *Cape May Wave* had columns like these, too.) One especially notable mention during the Mount Vernon years appeared late in the summer of 1891, describing sightings of U.S. president Benjamin Harrison on the Mount Vernon beach: "President Harrison has been frequently seen over here and enjoys walking along the front and observing the various marine curiosities."[31] For several years during his presidency, Harrison and his family spent their summers in neighboring Cape May Point.

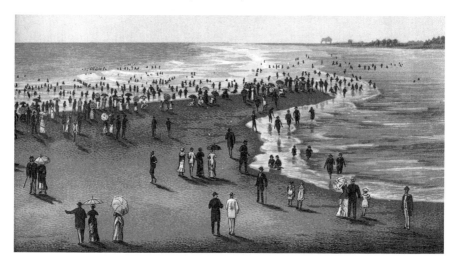

Detail from print showing view toward South Cape May and elephant building, circa 1885. *Courtesy of Robert Elwell Sr.*

In addition to fishing trips, hay rides and card parties hosted by the Buchholzes, Rutschmans and others, the local newspapers regularly noted news of residents arriving to set up their houses for the summer season, as well as the comings and goings of guests at the New Mount Vernon Hotel. Along with fishing and crabbing, hunting was a common activity. "Gunning is quite a favorite pastime for some of the guests of the New Mount Vernon… Snipe and yellow legs will have to be on their guard henceforth." Coverage even continued through the winter in the early days; consider this stern warning in February 1891: "Boys, beware how you break out windows in the New Mount Vernon Hotel, as we have our eyes on you." A summer news item reported on activity at the Eighth Avenue beach pavilion, "the favorite bathing spot of Mount Vernon beauties…During bathing hours here the pavilion is crowded by spectators who seem to enjoy looking on as much as the bathers do being admired." There was outdoor musical entertainment, too—an organ grinder and monkey—reported with language reflecting the times: "The first Dago and de monk of the season was working Mount Vernon cottagers with a grind organ, full of such tunes as 'Home Sweet Home,' 'Mikado,' 'Climbing Up the Golden Stairs,' and 'Annie Rooney.'"[32]

A two-column-long season-end article appeared on page one of an October 1893 *Star of the Cape*, penned collectively by members of an anonymous family, including their already nostalgic description of local farmers and immigrant hucksters who visited the community selling food: "Oh, for once more to hear in the early sunlight those bright and inspiring, as well as poetical, words of 'broadht,' 'broadht,' and then a mighty chorus from a semi-sleeping mob, crying, 'Mom, there's the bread man!'" The family's reports also reflected late nineteenth-century attitudes about the curative powers of fresh air, the mother noting, "I have never felt in better health than I do at the present time. I think that this summer's outing has added days to my life." Her son joined in: "I cannot help but believe that I am in better health and better off all around for having enjoyed the associations and breathed the fine air of the Cape."[33]

Besides the local Cape May newspapers, the press in Philadelphia and Trenton, New Jersey, reported on some of the community's activities in detail. The *Philadelphia Inquirer* reported on the incorporation of South Cape May: "The settlement of Mount Vernon, which was a part of West Cape May, could not get the beach protection it wanted, and…succeeded in having an election whereby they secured a separation from West Cape May. They propose to incorporate under the name of South Cape May, and expect ultimately to become a part of Cape May City." The *Inquirer* also reported on an inaugural celebration of the borough's founding, with the headline, "South Cape May Formally Opened," and noted, "South Cape May, as Mount Vernon is hereafter to be known, gave Cape May an Asbury Park and Ocean Grove appearance today. The Union Auditorium was opened to the public and a large audience attended."[34]

Much less celebratory coverage of borough events is found in the *Inquirer* in the following year, when it reported on April 23 about grand jury indictments against South Cape May's mayor, James Ritchie Jr., and borough resident Katie Bohm for "criminal intimacy" and another indictment against Mrs. Bohm's husband, Henry, for "keeping a disorderly house" in the borough. Some years later, in 1904, another story quoted Ritchie's wife, Elizabeth Adams Ritchie, describing her husband as "insanely jealous," threatening to divorce him and explaining that (despite her husband's claims) her recent disappearance had not involved another man.[35]

The local newspapers also devoted attention to various roadway improvements and similar developments. In the fall of 1890, Samuel Ewing was contracted to build a jetty on the Mount Vernon tract.[36] There were a number of references over the years to the "Missing Link"—the unfinished portion of Mount Vernon Avenue between Seventh Avenue in South Cape May and Second Avenue in Cape May City, which wasn't completed until 1926, although the link to Cape May Point had been completed long before, in 1891.

Athletic events and other spectacles were popular topics in the press, as well. Local boys formed the South Cape May Athletic Club, holding footraces and discus throws. There was an in-depth report on a series of quarter-mile bicycle races held on the South Cape May beach between Theo Fenn Jr., Donald Quantrell and Charles Ervin, in addition to the more formal games of the South Cape May baseball team. Another public spectacle of note was the sighting of a sea turtle weighing about eighty pounds that washed up on the beach. This was clearly topped, though, when the *Philadelphia Inquirer* reported that an escaped circus bear had been frolicking on the South Cape May beach before being lassoed with a borrowed clothesline and brought back to the circus.[37]

THE STORMS

The storms go back virtually to the very beginning. On January 30, 1891, when the first homes were still under construction, the *Star of the Cape* reported, "one of the unfinished houses of the Mt. Vernon settlement was blown from its foundation in the storm of last Saturday night." Not long after the 1894 incorporation of the borough, the *Philadelphia Inquirer* reported on an October 1896 nor'easter that badly tore up both South Cape May and Cape May Point, with tides reaching the first floor of several houses, some of which were washed entirely off their foundations. "The avenue in front of the beach from the east end of South Cape May to the Carleton House, at Cape May Point, is almost entirely washed away, the boardwalks are demolished and bath houses smashed into kindling wood."[38]

The next year was worse. First, a February nor'easter hit the South Jersey coast, uprooting trees across Cape May and completely submerging the train tracks in the meadows. The houses of South Cape May were entirely surrounded by water. Then, in October, a "tropical gale" hit with fifty-mile-an-hour winds, "the heaviest for nineteen years...The vice-like grip was sustained for three consecutive days in full force, accompanied by tremendous seas and high tides, which broke through the dead inlets of East Cape May and Mt. Vernon beaches, flooding the meadows and forcing the back water into the streets contiguous to them." The *Philadelphia Inquirer* reported that at South Cape May "the tide swept around the cottages, carrying away outhouses, bath houses and fences, and undermining three of the cottages."[39]

Within two years of the 1897 storm—in January 1899—state-elected officials began an effort to incorporate together Cape May City, West Cape May,

South Cape May and Cape May Point. On March 19, the paper mentioned this again, describing planned improvements that would be made possible by joining forces: "One of the improvements contemplated is the erection of sea walls for the protection of the entire territory, the sea front of which is about eight miles in extent." There were no further reports on this effort that year.[40]

South Cape May was spared from major storms at this time and for a few more years, until the borough and Cape May Point both sustained considerable damage from a storm that hit at one o'clock in the morning of November 24, 1901, taking a good slice of Beach Avenue out to sea.[41]

Much worse, though, was 1903, a year when three big storms hit South Cape May hard. First was a nor'easter that hit the area in April with a "perfect deluge of rain." South Cape May, in particular, fared badly. "The heavy seas made great inroads over the tract, carrying with them tons of sand from the hills lining the ocean front and depositing it in the rear of the railroad tracks connecting this resort with Cape May Point. Two houses were washed from their underpinning and were partially wrecked." Unoccupied at the time, the homes belonged to the Lynch and Netter families. Also badly damaged were the trolley tracks, with about two thousand feet washed entirely from their foundations.[42]

Then, in mid-September, the tail end of a storm that had been raging in the South and West hit Cape May. A pier very close to South Cape May, the Queen Anne, constructed to serve as a landing for rail passengers from Baltimore, Washington and other points, "was almost entirely swept away and pieces of the wreckage are strewn along the beach from Broadway to Cape May Point. Only a few of the timbers near Beach Avenue now remain to show that the place was ever occupied by an ocean pier nearly 1,100 feet long…Several bath houses in South Cape May were overturned and the streets and pavements everywhere strewn with leaves and branches from the trees."[43]

The final storm that year arrived in early October. "A heavy northeast wind has driven in the greatest tide seen here for many years. The meadows look like a raging sea." South Cape May was inundated, and the property of borough resident David Sykes was "washed down by the sea."[44]

The winter of 1917–18 had a severe impact on the Cape May area and much of the Northeast overall, with record snowfall in January and record low temperatures throughout the winter. Among the major storms in the surrounding region that winter was the Knickerbocker Storm of January 27–28, named for the Knickerbocker Theater in Washington, D.C., whose roof collapsed in the blizzard, killing ninety-three people. Railroad lines between

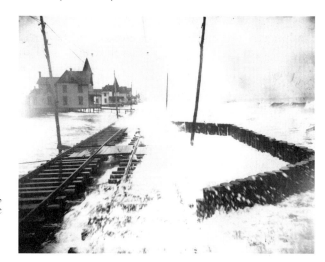

South Cape May beachfront during storm, from photo dating before 1909. *Photo by Isaac B. Zwalley. Courtesy of H. Gerald MacDonald.*

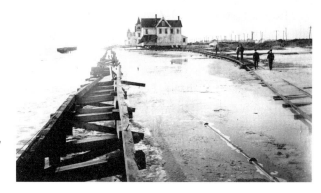

Aftermath of storm at South Cape May, with trolley tracks knocked entirely off their footings, before 1909. *Photo by Isaac B. Zwalley. Courtesy of H. Gerald MacDonald.*

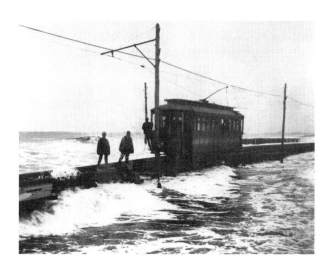

Electric trolley along South Cape May beach. *Photo by Isaac B. Zwalley. Courtesy of H. Gerald MacDonald.*

Washington and Philadelphia were covered by three feet of snow, with drifts as high as sixteen feet. January 1918 was the coldest month on record in New Jersey up until that time, with temperatures twenty to thirty degrees below normal during its first week. The mean temperature for Cape May in January was less than twenty-six degrees and still at freezing for the month of February. There was also considerable snowfall in Cape May in 1918—more than twenty inches—but what made this particularly harsh was the impact of the cold, which prevented thawing and kept the ground covered for many more consecutive days than usual. Ice formed to great thicknesses in harbors, frost entered deep into the ground and water mains and pipes in buildings froze.[45]

The relocation of the homes of the Bailie and Weinmann families to the western end of Cape May City not long after that very severe winter was a clear indication that South Cape May's potential as a thriving beach community was gone. Within a few more years, there was another sign as well. By then, the reports of bicycle races on the beach, card-playing parties and fishing trips by South Cape May neighbors didn't make it into the local newspaper anymore, but there were several pages devoted to South Cape May in the fall of 1923: legal notices of a tax sale of hundreds of lots in the borough, owing to delinquent taxes.[46] It was as if someone had finally come to his senses and realized that all those many lots that the Mount Vernon Land Company sold in its heyday—before it became the South Cape May Land Company—were never going to be developed, and the borough was never going to collect a cent of taxes on them.

A Ghost Town

While the 1923 tax sale announcements may have been a final signal for the end of South Cape May's flourishing, there was a foreshadowing notice in the *Star of the Cape* shortly after the 1903 storms that was especially startling. The January 9, 1904 issue contained a prominent, front-page article that stands as the most detailed account of a single South Cape May evening, with the headline: "Ghost on the Beach." In stark contrast to reports of the comings and goings of the borough's Philadelphia society residents, an anonymous writer describes his walk from Cape May Point to Cape May City, where he comes upon a ghost in an abandoned house in South Cape May, one that has been damaged in the storms. A captivating, suspenseful piece, it's included here almost in its entirety to end this section on South Cape May history through the early twentieth century.

New Year's Eve—Last Thursday evening—I had occasion to walk from Cape May Point to this City. I tarried at the particular place where I was spending the evening rather late, perhaps later than good manners would seem to permit; but it was the last night of the old year...which I think you will agree with me was a creditable excuse...It was past midnight when I started homeward. I was all alone. The night was very still...I looked up at the quiet stars and the half moon a long while. I listened to the roar of the sea, faint and melancholy a quarter of a mile or so distant. There was no other sound; no sign of life. At night the sea has a strange fascination. There is mystery about it...

While I was listening to the roar of the sea, a strange thing happened. The ocean seemed to be approaching, the sound of the breakers becoming louder and louder. I shall never be able to explain intelligibly the state of my feelings...as though I had been held up from the earth and left in the air by some intangible support, while the sea came to me.

Anyhow, all of a sudden a wave washed quite over my shoetops. I jumped at the shock of the icy water. This must have had the effect of bringing me to my senses for I now realized that I was standing on the shore of the ocean...

It was flood tide, and I kept close to the edge of the waves. On my right the sea was quite calm in the soft moonlight. On my left was the still, still shore—the closed houses, wrapped up in the shimmering light of the moon, haunted with their ghostly shadows.

...I was just approaching that cottage which the sea undermined, you remember, and toppled over slightly, breaking most of the windows and window shutters, throwing down the chimney, twisting the whole house and tearing out the parlor, and leaving the whole cottage a hopeless wreck. By the way, it reminds one of the house in Scripture.

I was just emerging from the shadow of the house just below this poor wrecked one, when I was startled by a shrieking cry.

"Help! Help!! H-e-l-p!!"

I stopped dead. My heart stopped. Everything stopped. Then I gathered myself together and looked—up and down the beach, out to sea, to the right, to the left, up into the sky. Nothing stirred. Nothing moved. Not a sound.

I took a step or two, and again my blood froze.

"Help! Help!! Help!!!" came the voice.

I now perceived the form of a human being in the upper window of the wrecked cottage. It was making frantic gesticulations, and throwing out its arms in the wildest possible manner, while at intervals came the terrified

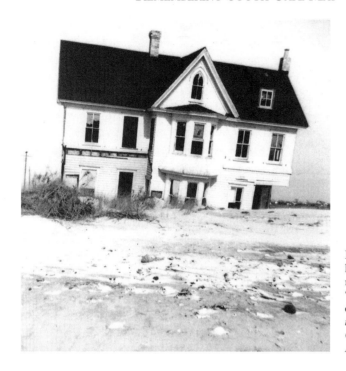

Former Rutschman home, circa 1950s, reminiscent of the "hopeless wreck" described in the *Star of the Cape*, January 1904. *Courtesy of Robert W. Elwell Sr.*

shriek for help. In a moment it disappeared. All was quiet. I was all in the most distressing tremble you ever imagined or dreamed or read of. How was I to get home? Pass the house, or strike off across the meadows to the Turnpike?…I have a good deal of prying curiosity in my make-up and I never believed in ghosts. I determined to make sure whether there was anybody in that house. So with a mighty effort, I shouted.

"Is anyone there?"

I started at the echo of my own voice. But no answer came. After a few moments I took a step, perhaps a dozen of the most cautious steps I have ever taken in my life—toward the house and the window where the figure had appeared. Then I grasped up a handful of pebbles and threw them chattering against the side of the cottage and in at the window. Then all was still again—as still as still. The very sea held its breath. That was enough. I shot off across the meadows like a rifle ball, and never once looked back.

The reference midway through to the South Cape May house that "reminds one of the house in Scripture" is, no doubt, a reference to the one mentioned in Paul's second letter to the Ephesians, which was "doomed to fall."

From the 1920s to the Present:

A Firsthand Account

CHAPTER 5

A Family's Start in
South Cape May

MY GRANDPARENTS IN 1923

Part II of this book, moving from the 1920s down to the present, draws largely from my own recollections and observations of life in South Cape May, while also noting some major events covered in the press—specifically, the mentions of floods and storm damage in the borough. There are several reasons for this shift. For one, the written record of South Cape May after the early 1920s isn't as extensive as for the earlier years. The local newspapers didn't carry gossipy weekly news reports on the borough like the ones that had appeared in the early years. There's no cache of building contracts made with noted architects. Also, given the considerable representation of the Burcher family in South Cape May over three generations, there is much about the family's experiences that is representative of life in the borough. And, finally, I haven't yet found any other living longtime residents of the borough outside my family who could add details from their own experiences.

One of my first recollections of South Cape May is of visiting my grandparents there at their little cottage when I was about three years old, about 1926. I remember standing in front of the little place and saluting the flag every morning. John Samuel Burcher, my grandfather on my father's side, bought his property in South Cape May in August 1923, four months before I was born and before the big delinquent tax sale of borough

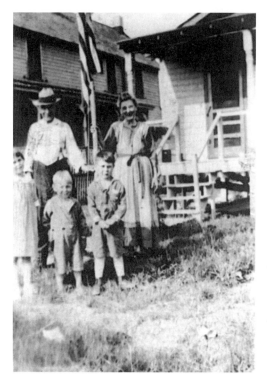

John Samuel Burcher and Clara Strepple Burcher at the South Cape May cottage with grandchildren Teresa, Joseph (the author) and Francis, circa 1926. *Author's collection.*

properties. He purchased two lots for $90, and he hired a carpenter to build his small cottage for $800.[47] It was a very modest dwelling, just one story with a little pitched roof, not unlike my own cottage on Sunset Boulevard today. In fact, it was not much bigger than my main room, maybe eighteen by twelve feet—very small.

Born in Bermuda in 1847, John Samuel Burcher came to the United States as an infant when his parents, Eliza and John Burcher, a blacksmith, immigrated to Philadelphia. My grandfather served in the Union army, joining at the age of eighteen at the very end of the Civil War, assigned to the 214th Infantry Regiment of Pennsylvania.[48] A few years after the war, he was back in Philadelphia living with his parents on Delaware Avenue, two doors away from the Strepple family, which included my grandmother, Clara, and my great-aunt Jennie. Soon after, John Samuel Burcher was working in Philadelphia in a boat-building business with his brother James, who had been an apprentice boat builder from the time he was sixteen and who worked in that trade for the rest of his life, together with his sons. By 1910, my grandfather was working as a watchman for the Philadelphia Navy Yard, which saw a flurry of activity in the years during and immediately after World War I, with a workforce of twelve thousand building huge warships and planes.[49] He kept that job into his seventies, through the 1920s.

It seems likely that by 1923, when my grandfather bought his property in South Cape May, he was retired from the navy yard, considering that he was seventy-six years old at that time. The navy yard cut its workforce drastically by 1921, down to six thousand employees, and by then, he might have put in enough years to collect a pension, combining it with a small pension from his Civil War service, so that he could afford to spend the rest of his summers in South Cape May instead of in the heat of Philadelphia. He and my grandmother bought their two lots in the borough from Alfred and Elizabeth Rudolph. The property was on Eighth Avenue, just north of the intersection with Mount Vernon Avenue.

VIRGINIA GARDINER: GREAT-AUNT JENNIE

A few years after my grandparents were set up in South Cape May, in September 1927, my great-aunt Jennie bought her own property in

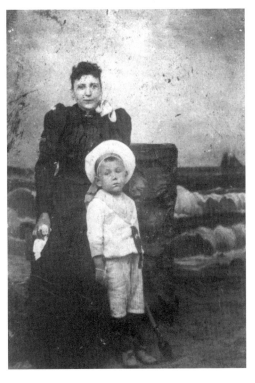

Clara Strepple Burcher with young boy in photo with seaside backdrop. *Author's collection.*

the borough—a much more substantial house, the one originally built for Thomas D. Caswell and his family in 1893 by the contractors Church and Elwell. A handsome, two-and-a-half-story building near the ocean, about two blocks from my grandparents' cottage, it was similar to some of the others built there in the early 1890s, such as the Rutschman and Miller homes, and it's likely the architect was Enos Williams.[50] Divorced at the time she bought the house, Aunt Jennie, who was my grandmother Clara Burcher's sister, purchased it from another single woman, Annie Dedrick, a widow from Philadelphia. Aunt Jennie didn't hold on to the house long, though.

Aunt Jennie had an interesting background, probably somewhat typical of some of the people who settled in South Cape May in the 1920s. Her name appears as Virginia Gardiner on her South Cape May deed; she was married at one time to William J. Gardiner. Jennie had at least one child, my father's cousin Myrtle, possibly two, but I don't remember them making visits with her to South Cape May when I was young. As a young girl, in the

69

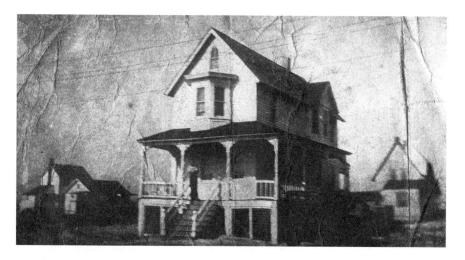

The Burcher family home on Ninth Avenue in South Cape May, circa 1933. *Author's collection.*

1880s, Jennie and her sisters Clara and Emma were living in Philadelphia with their single mother, Margaret, a housekeeper; their father had died or left the family by then. The girls were all working as "book folders," doing the handwork needed for book binderies in the days before assembly was more fully automated. Aunt Jennie was still doing related work in 1920 in Philadelphia, when she was in her sixties, after her husband was gone and not long before she bought her house in South Cape May.[51]

My sister-in-law, Dorothy Burcher, wife of my oldest brother, Ed, recalls that Aunt Jennie got the idea of buying a good-sized house in the borough as a way to make some extra income by renting out rooms for the summer. This didn't really pan out, though. By August 1933, she couldn't make her mortgage payments to the Stone Harbor Building and Loan, and that month my father took possession of the house, agreeing to take over the mortgage. Aunt Jennie was afraid to bring up the idea of my father taking over the house while my grandmother was in earshot, for fear of upsetting her. In 1933, my grandmother was known to be a bit eccentric—she kept a loaded rifle in her bedroom—although it's understandable that she would have been sensitive, since that was the year my grandfather died. So Aunt Jennie put her request to my father in writing, saying she had just received her mortgage bill and couldn't pay it and asking him to take over the property. "I'm sorry to seem to force you to take it, as I know you do not want it, but you may be able to get something out of it." Of course, this was at the height of the Great Depression. Still, it amazes me that my father might have been reluctant to take over that wonderful place just one house in from the beach because he'd have to take on a loan for $1,000.

My Parents and Their Twelve Children

My father, Edgar Francis Burcher Sr., regularly took his whole growing family down to South Cape May to visit with our grandparents and Aunt Jennie well before he took over Aunt Jennie's house. I don't know exactly how long we stayed there or whether we were there for regular weekend visits or for a week or two at a time. I remember my grandfather puttering around; he must have been over eighty years old by then. There wasn't much for him to do. He might walk down to the beach and back. I have a clearer recollection of staying in South Cape May in the summers after my father took over Aunt Jennie's house, when I was ten years old. My parents would sometimes take us there as early as May, and we wouldn't return to Berlin, New Jersey, where we were living, until September. Usually, though, we'd go down about June 15, when we were done picking crops on our farm, and not come back until mid-September, when we'd sell corn.

Just as we'd spend summers as children in South Cape May, my father spent some of his boyhood summers away from his Philadelphia home, staying with his uncles in the farm area of Bucks County, Pennsylvania, where he got to know a little about farming. But farming wasn't his main occupation. He started out in business at fifteen years old, selling fire escapes. Later, he got a certificate in structural engineering from the Drexel Institute of Art, Science and Industry (which later became Drexel University). He answered a newspaper ad for a job as a designer with Berko Brothers, a firm that built structural steel, eventually moving up to become president of the company. He traveled into Philadelphia every day except Sundays to the Berko Brothers plant, not far from Independence Hall and the Benjamin Franklin Bridge, sometimes by train but mostly by car, especially in the summer, when he'd be with us in South Cape May on weekends.

He was raised a Baptist but converted to Catholicism when he married my mother, at her insistence—something he did willingly, and he embraced the faith completely. Christened Theresa M. Waters, my mother was called Tess or Tessie and came from a family of ten children, whereas my father was an only child. Her parents were Irish immigrants. Her father, James Waters, arrived in Philadelphia as a young man about 1870, working briefly as a

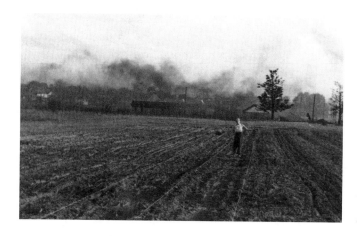

Theresa Burcher in the family's strawberry patch on their farm in Berlin, New Jersey, 1945. *Author's collection.*

laborer, then as a saloonkeeper and finally, for many years, as a boilermaker for Baldwin Locomotive Works, the largest steam locomotive manufacturer in the United States, which produced the steam locomotive used on the train lines that crossed the Mount Vernon tract in the late nineteenth century.

My father bought our farm in Berlin, about twenty miles outside of Philadelphia and the Berko Brothers, sometime before 1920—fifteen acres, with two houses, including a sharecropper house. The farm was a big focus for us, and we would stay home from school to do the planting and picking at various points in the year. My parents had seven children by the time I was born in 1923 and twelve altogether by 1935, nine sons and three daughters. Like most of my brothers and sisters, I was born in December, which meant that my mother was three to six months pregnant for many of those summers in South Cape May, with a six- to nine-month-old infant in the house.

No matter how much my father loved to think of himself as a gentleman farmer, he didn't really know much about farming. He wouldn't spend money to buy a new tractor, have a cow examined or get the fertilizer he needed. The horse died. The cow died. The pigs died. He was more adept as a beekeeper and had great hives, but we never sold a pound of honey. One night, a thief stole fourteen of his hives. Still, we had a number of relatively successful crops: strawberries, corn, potatoes and other vegetables. We didn't sell much of what we grew, but the farm did help provide food for the family, especially during the Depression. As an interesting parallel, older year-round residents of the Cape May area tell me that hunting small game in the meadows of South Cape May in the off-season is what helped their families through the Depression.

From Berlin to Cape May was about seventy-five miles, and the drive down in our 1928 Buick probably took three to five hours. My father would

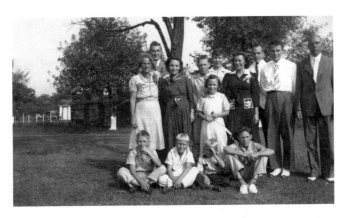

Burcher family, 1940. *Standing*: Theresa, Jim, Claire, Joseph, Rita, Francis, Teresa, John, Edgar Jr., Edgar Sr. *Sitting*: Dick, Paul, Vincent, Walter. *Author's collection*.

come down on Saturday afternoon and leave on Monday morning or Sunday night. He would carry multiple spare tires to cover all the blowouts he was sure to have on the journey. There weren't any garages around, and the roads weren't well maintained; many of the local ones were gravel. The car broke down in Mays Landing once, and my father had to walk five miles to get help. We children weren't fazed, though. We unloaded the car with my mother, spread out in a farmer's meadow and had a picnic. My father was very staid and self-controlled, and I rarely saw him get rattled, even though there were many things for him to get rattled about with all those children in that car. It was an ordeal just to get to South Cape May.

In a sense, my father and mother were quite affluent for their time, with a summer place in South Cape May and a farm with two houses on it in Berlin. But the Depression wasn't easy at all, especially with a family of our size. Around that time, hoboes would come around to our house in Berlin, see us sitting at the dinner table and knock on the window or the door for handouts. We fed quite a number of hoboes. My mother and father also took in people who needed help. One family, the Cudeyros, from Spain, virtually lived with us from about 1930 onward, and they came to South Cape May also. I got home from kindergarten one day and told my mother about a boy in my class, Tommy Cudeyro, who didn't have any shoes. She asked me to bring him home the next day. Tommy's mother had died, and his father, Pete, a carpenter, was raising the family by himself, having a difficult time. Ultimately, they moved into our sharecropper house and practically rebuilt it. They were also a big help in repairing Aunt Jennie's old South Cape May house in 1933, staying with us there while they built extra supports and did structural work, reinforcing all the timbers underneath to make it strong enough to stand up to the Cape May storms, at least for a while.

CHAPTER 6

Playing and Working the Beaches Around South Cape May

ON THE BEACH WITH NEIGHBORS AND FAMILY

As young children, we didn't really seem to live in our South Cape May house much at all. We spent much of our time on the beach, playing in the pale, tan-colored sand, around the few grassy dunes and in the water—cold in the early summer months but warm by August. It wasn't crowded or especially noisy, aside from the noise *we* made. With us there were just our local neighbors and some extra visitors on weekends, fifty people at most along that mile of beach, and no lifeguards. We'd be in the house at night and on rainy days, and once we were in, my mother kept the screen door locked. It was crowded with our big family, even though the house was a good size. All twelve children weren't down there all the time, though. Ed was working in Philadelphia for the stock market, and Claire was a hairdresser. John went into the CCC (Civilian Conservation Corps), one of Roosevelt's New Deal work programs, when he was sixteen, before he joined the air force.

We'd spend our days in bathing suits my mother made out of old woolen sweaters—not a great feeling on the body while up on the sand after being in the ocean. There were many more mosquitoes than today, although the Mosquito Control Commission was supposedly doing a great amount of work in the area; one of the longtime South Cape May residents, O.W. Lafferty, worked for the commission.[52] I don't recall that work being very

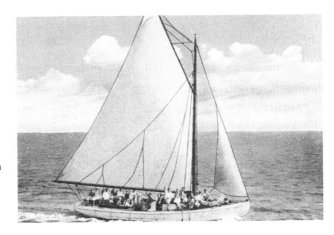

The *Polly Page II*, which sailed past South Cape May beach daily, circa 1930. *Courtesy of Don Pocher.*

effective, though. We'd burn cattails all around the house at night to try to drive the mosquitoes away.

The game we most liked playing on the beach was something we called "cannonball." At low tide, we went out into the bogs—it was all very marshy there—and made big mud balls, rolling them in the sand and setting them out in the sun to dry. It would be my brothers Franny, Walt, Dick and I, along with children from the other houses, such as Frankie and Marie Megenedy. We'd choose up sides and then build sand forts, charge at the other side and hit one another with these things. Cattails were other ammunition—soaked in seawater—and we'd throw them with all our might.

We'd swim out from the beach to the *Polly Page*, a single-mast sloop that would take vacationers around the Cape every day. It would come promptly at ten o'clock in the morning. We would try to get up as close as we could to it and beg for money, calling out, "Throw us a dime!"

I don't think anyone ever drowned on the South Cape May beach, but we did have one close call. When he was about eight or nine years old, my brother Dick got caught in a riptide, what we called a "sea puss." I ran in from the water and yelled to my sister Teresa, "Trese! Dick's drowning!" The riptide was taking him down. We both ran in and held him up. We knew that there was a good chance we could go under with him, and we were completely panicked. So we were screaming, hollering and waving to people on the beach. They just waved back at us! As if they were waving to the *Polly Page*! Nobody came to help. I don't know how we did it, but somehow, we all got back to safety.

On the beach, we'd also gather up dunnage—that is, lumber that would wash up from the sea. My father would always find some use for it and asked us to grab it before our enterprising neighbor, Bill Fisner, did. Freighters would dump out big four-by-four beams from crates that were empty at the end of their runs, and they would float up on our beach. Other times, we'd get lumber from boats that smashed up and washed ashore. My brother John, home from the CCC, was dismembering a big barge that had floated in one day and had four-by-twelve side timbers. He held a plank up over his head; it had two huge nails as big as my finger hanging off it. The plank slipped out of his hands, and he got impaled by a spike that went right through his foot. I was alone with him, about ten years old. He said, "Joe, get Mr. Wagner," the man who worked for the borough fixing the roads, electricity and other things. I ran up to the borough community hall, on Tenth Street, where he was, and he jumped in his Model T Ford, bringing a tool kit and a towel. We got down to John, and Mr. Wagner got a crowbar out. He said to John, "I'm going to leverage it up, John. When I do, I want you to fall backward and wrap the towel around your foot." I can't remember anything but blood and the towel. John was lucky his foot wasn't paralyzed.

OTHER FAMILIES, THE OBLATES AND A VACATION BOARDINGHOUSE

A number of our neighbors in South Cape May had children around my age. The Guensheimers across the street from us on Ninth Avenue had two young boys who later attended LaSalle College prep school. Next door to them was the Thistler family, right on the beach, with young Albert and Catherine. Also in the neighborhood were the Moyers, but their parents absolutely forbade their children to play with us—not with our mudball fights and other nonsense. Behind our next-door neighbors, the Watsons, were the O'Sheas on Eighth Avenue. We used to dig tunnels in the sand deep enough to get under their house, next to their floorboards, just out of mischief, even smoking cigarettes under there. Mrs. O'Shea would pound on the floor. "I hear you kids under there! Get out!"

Behind our house and next to the O'Sheas on Eighth Avenue was the Megenedy family and my summer girlfriend, Marie. I remember running along the beach with her. Other diversions available to us were dances at Convention Hall on the boardwalk in Cape May City. Friday nights, they had dances for children early in the evening and a talent show, with tap dancing and singing. Wednesday nights, the girls dressed up in evening gowns. Before World War II, no one went to the boardwalk at night unless they were dressed up a bit. Men wore linen jackets and ties. The Megenedys later sold their house to the Goggins, a family my sister Rita married into.

The families in the borough were mainly Protestant and included at least one minister, Reverend Logan—although Logan might have been his first name. Our other fellow Catholics included the Guensheimers, O'Sheas, Megenedys and Kellys. We'd see one another at mass either at Our Lady Star of the Sea in Cape May City or St. Agnes at Cape May Point. The largest group of Catholics in South Cape May was the Oblates of St. Francis de Sales, a religious order from Philadelphia and Wilmington, Delaware, who had a summer retreat in the borough, headquartered at the old South Cape May Hotel. They were mainly young men who had just graduated from high school, beginning to study for the priesthood. They'd come out on the beach, toss a ball around and play with us. One of them—Father Walter Kelly—was a great friend of the family who loved baseball and became a teacher at Northeast Catholic High School in Philadelphia.

Although the Oblates monopolized the South Cape May Hotel, there was still a place for vacationers to stay in South Cape May for short visits: the house that belonged to the Kelly family, which was another of the early South Cape May homes, originally owned by John Wilson. The Kellys operated what would be a bed-and-breakfast today but was more of a vacation boardinghouse. Shortly after my brother Ed and his wife, Dot, were married and their first children came along, they used to stay at the Kellys' for a week or so at a time, until Ed built his own cottage next to my grandfather's old place. Dot recalls the Kelly house as having an unusual setup. Each family

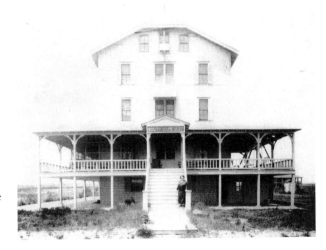

South Cape May Hotel, circa 1920s, where the Oblates of St. Francis de Sales later held summer retreats. *Courtesy of Robert W. Elwell Sr.*

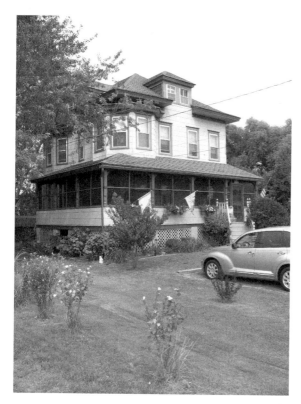

Left: Former Kelly/Wilson home at 603 Sunset Boulevard, 2006. *Photograph by Robert Kenselaar.*

Below: Edgar F. Burcher Jr. (left) building his family's cottage on Eighth Avenue in South Cape May. *Courtesy of Dorothy Burcher.*

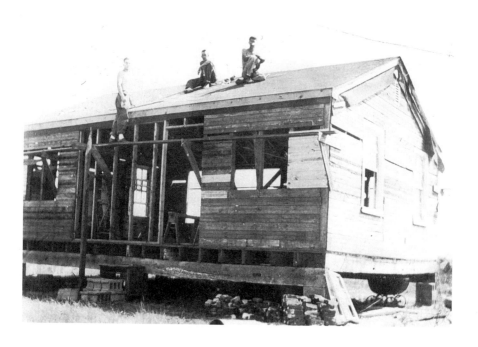

had a bedroom and cooking privileges on the ground floor, which seemed more like a basement. There were four kitchens with kerosene stoves and little sets of tables and chairs, and there were stairs from there up to the main entrance and the porch above. There were no living rooms, but there was space available on the porches, with rocking chairs.

Looking out from the porch and seeing my grandfather's old house gave Ed the idea of building his own cottage, constructing it in sections back home in Berlin and carting those sections down to South Cape May in a truck he borrowed from Berko Brothers. Once he brought the sections down, he had the family help assemble them, bolting them together, and from then on, Dot and her four daughters would spend the whole summer in South Cape May, with Ed coming down on weekends and staying for a week or two, just as my father had done.

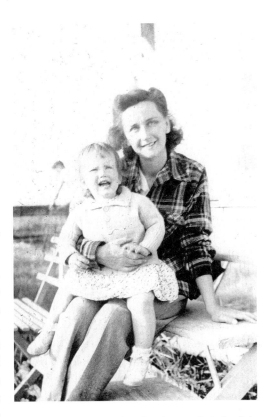

Dorothy Burcher with her daughter at their family's cottage in South Cape May, late 1940s. *Courtesy of Dorothy Burcher.*

HOME-COOKED MEALS AND MODERN CONVENIENCES

For breakfast, we always had oatmeal, homemade bread and butter. My mother would make four loaves of bread every day. She sent us out on the beach with peanut butter and jelly sandwiches for lunch. In the afternoon, she took a nap with the door locked. An insurance man, Mr. Seiner, would visit the neighborhood, collecting ten cents a week on insurance policies. He'd knock on the door, and she would curse him out for waking her up. Nobody came near the house between one and three o'clock.

During the day, if we had to use the toilet, we just went right in the sand dunes. There was plumbing in the houses; they had fresh running water that came in from Mount Vernon Avenue, but there was no sewer system for the community, only septic tanks. We had toilet facilities in the house, although at first we had outhouses.

For dinner, my mother made tremendous soups, which we thrived on. She was also the original Paul Prudhomme, the television chef known for his blackened fish dishes. If you gave my mother a fish, you'd never see the white meat. It would have a deep, thick, almost black crust on it. I remember very distinctly one particular fish dinner. I was up, as usual, at six o'clock in the morning. I was probably the earliest riser in the house. I went down to the beach and saw an osprey dive into the water. I knew it was going to get a fish, so I picked up the biggest clamshell I could find, and as soon as the bird got the fish, I threw that shell at the osprey with everything I had. Sure enough, it dropped the fish right down, a huge one. I brought it home to my mother, and she said, "God works in mysterious ways!" And she fried it up that night, New Orleans style by way of South Cape May.

As far as modern conveniences, we didn't have many at all, beyond our kerosene stove. My father refused for the longest time to have a phone in South Cape May, or in Berlin, for that matter. He would use the phone at community hall in South Cape May or a neighbor's phone. There was radio in those days, of course, but we didn't have one down there. People ask me what we did for entertainment in the evening. Some of the things we did were exciting and even dangerous.

Rumrunners

From time to time at night, we would sneak out of the house through the window on our second floor, crawl onto the porch roof and slide down the porch side beams—we were second-story escape artists. We'd shinny down and jump onto a sand dune near the house and, later, shinny back up again. Skulking around in the dunes in the moonlight, we would smoke cigarettes and roast up some potatoes (which we stole from our back porch) on fires we made of driftwood, sticks and dried seaweed. We'd light up some cattail to keep the mosquitoes away and roast marshmallows sometimes, if we could steal those, too.

It was a bit more dangerous than it sounds, because of the rumrunners. This was in the days of Prohibition, when alcohol was completely banned in the United States, from the 1920s to the early '30s. Rumrunners used to come down to the South Cape May beach, which was much more isolated than the beach in Cape May City, and they would drive huge Chevy trucks down on the beach as far as they could past our house on Ninth Avenue, always at night. Rowboats would come in. They'd unload the kegs and crates into wheelbarrows, push them up from the sandy beach to the hard road and then load the trucks up with the alcohol and take off.

The Coast Guard would be on the lookout for the rumrunners. Charlie Roseman, a chief petty officer, was involved in this work. His family had been in the Cape May area from the 1700s; they were boat builders and operated Roseman's Boat Yard, which is still in operation today. Charlie was captain of one of the Coast Guard boats that patrolled after the rumrunners. He and his men would get up close to the beach in their boat and fire five-inch shells at them. They took their job very seriously, because the rumrunners were in violation of federal law. We witnessed some of these skirmishes from the dunes at night, after we snuck out of the house. We'd also find empty bottles and broken glass the rumrunners left after scrambling out when the Coast Guard came after them. The Coast Guardsmen would patrol the beach, too, and if they found a crate of beer, wine or whiskey, they would smash it up. That scene in the dark, late at night on the South Cape May beach, is what stays in my mind most of all, though. It was dangerous but exciting for us to see.

Working Around the Area

Although I've said that we spent a lot of our time on the beach, we also had plenty of work to do, and we held jobs in the Cape May area from the time we were young. One of the assignments my mother gave me was beachcombing—walking the beach from South Cape May to the Admiral Hotel, Cape May's huge, magnificent brick hotel, about two and a half miles away, at the city's eastern end.

My brother Dick, five years younger than me, was my companion. "Out the door!" my mother would command. "It's time to go beachcombing!" We'd pick up anything that looked usable, with an eye out especially for towels and wallets. Any money in a wallet was fair game, but we would turn the wallets in if they had driver's licenses in them. We'd find rings, packages and eyeglasses. But mostly, we were looking for towels. There was nearly always an infant in the house, and my mother needed diapers. We'd bring home towels, and she would make diapers out of them.

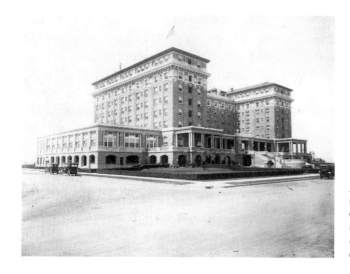

Admiral Hotel at
the eastern end of
Cape May City.
*Courtesy of Cape May
County Historical and
Genealogical Society.*

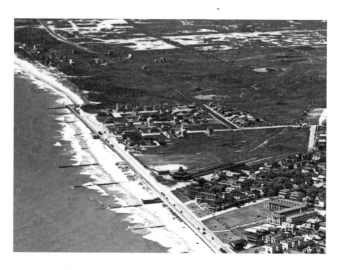

View looking west,
1932. South Cape
May is at top left.
South Broadway and
nearby Cape May
streets are at center.
*Courtesy of Cape May
County Historical and
Genealogical Society.*

Later in the day, I'd work with the huckster who sold fruits and vegetables through our streets, Mr. Lepore. I'd wait for his truck on Eighth Avenue and jump on board, going up and down the streets, asking people if they wanted string beans or whatever else. He would come through South Cape May, take me through Cape May Point and then drop me off. He paid me a dime or so and gave me a little bruised or damaged fruit.

Another mainstay of the neighborhood was the iceman, a wonderful, husky, handsome black man named Green. We didn't have a working relationship with him, like Mr. Lepore, but we'd follow Mr. Green's ice wagon around, watching him chip ice from 150-pound blocks and scoop it up into bags. He would give us some to suck on or make ice water with, which was a treat on a hot day. The people in the neighborhood would put signs in their windows to show how much ice they wanted, anywhere from 25 to 100 pounds of ice. He'd chip those blocks of ice down to the right size and lug them on a leather shoulder strap into each house, even if no one was home. My parents and the neighbors always left their doors open for him.

Another activity that kept us busy was cutting our neighbors' lawns—Mr. Patton, in particular. We didn't mow the lawns, though. With the tough sea grass, lawnmowers were useless—if we had even owned a lawnmower. We didn't have shears or other proper tools, either. We used hand scissors. It took hours, out in the open sun.

We also went on errands for our mother, always walking everywhere. With my father coming down to South Cape May in the old Buick mainly just on weekends, he wasn't there to drive us anywhere during the week. We didn't have bicycles. There was no taxi. There weren't many cars; you couldn't thumb a ride. There was one bus that came out of Cape May City, Church's Bus. Many of the places we went were not far away, though. Among the places we'd go often was Konowitch's Grocery, at Ocean and Washington Streets in Cape May City. Another store on Washington Street was Kokes's Bakery, which is now called La Patisserie. Ben Franklin's Five and Ten Cent

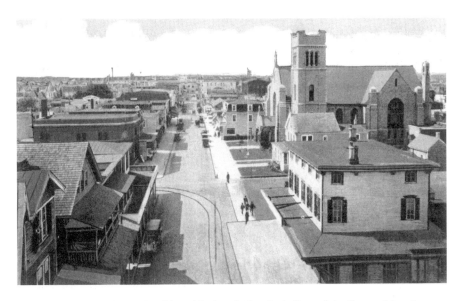

Washington Street, Cape May City, with church Our Lady Star of the Sea at right, circa 1920s. *Courtesy of Cape May County Historical and Genealogical Society.*

Store was there, too—right across from Dellas's Five and Ten, also still there. At the pool hall, you could get cigarettes, and there were plenty of drunks there and bookies who operated pretty much in the open. It was all much different than it is today—Washington Street is now a pedestrian mall, closed to traffic—but the same buildings are standing. Nearby on Jackson Street was Swain's Hardware, which is an institution in the Cape May area, founded in 1896 and still a major retailer for the community.

Once we got a little older, we'd also sell newspapers, the *Philadelphia Inquirer* in the morning and the *Philadelphia Ledger* in the afternoon and evening. I really hustled—up and down the streets, the boardwalk, outside church on Sunday mornings, even on the beach selling papers on hot afternoons. I'd sell them at the train stations, too, and take rides on the train to Wildwood and back to sell them. Cape May had two train stations in those days: the Pennsylvania Railroad Station, a magnificent terminal on Grant Street, near where Uncle Bill's Pancake House is today, and another station at Jackson Street, which is a bus stop now. The day-tripping fishermen from Philadelphia at the C-View Bar were good customers. It was a rough crowd, though. Some of those men would be out at sea, drinking beer all day and then continuing their drinking at the C-View. (It has a much nicer atmosphere now.) We sometimes got into serious fistfights with other tough Irish and Italian boys over who had the right to sell newspapers at what corner.

Caddying at the Cape May Golf Club was another line of work for us. It was a nine-hole course, situated where the Cape May elementary school is now, not especially impressive. There were no rolling hills and not a lot of trees or brush, although one of its features was Cape Island Creek, which ran from South Cape May through there. At first the caddies got twenty-five cents for working nine holes, until I formed a little caddies' union and moved it up to fifty cents.

Once in a while, my brothers and I would go from South Cape May down to the dock at Schellenger's Landing, the main harbor in Cape May City, to get fish. We weren't actually fishing, though. We were stealing fish off the big commercial fishing boats. Our brother Franny was a leader in this. We found a rowboat in disrepair somewhere and fixed it up; nobody seemed to be using it. We'd take it and hide under the dock with a net, and when the big boats came in, we'd grab some of the fish that fell into the water as they were unloading. We'd take those fish in a wagon down to Corgie Street, in back of the mansion on Lafayette, a private home at that time but now a hotel. We would sell the fish—ten cents each—to the household help who worked there or nearby, the black housemaids and cooks, many of whom were from

Baltimore or Washington. There was a sizable black community in Cape May in those days, and there was a segregated beach, with black lifeguards, over at Grant Street and Beach Avenue. Things weren't completely segregated, though; there were black caddies and newspaper boys who worked together with us.

Another great job I had later, when I was in my late teens, was working in the bowling alley, out on a crowded pier near Decatur and Beach Drive, which had an arcade and a carousel. The bowling alley was built over the ocean on pilings—eight lanes, mostly warped and almost concave, which helped the bowlers get high scores. We worked as pin setters. In those days, the process wasn't automated. Instead, my brothers Dick and Walt and I would sit above the end of the lane, setting up the pins, one by one. We'd help the bowlers out by slyly kicking extra pins down, in hopes of a tip. Sometimes a pin left standing would be on the far side of the lane, so it could be tough to kick it over, but we'd do our best—blow on it, wave our arms, whatever. It was great fun. We'd work from six o'clock in the evening until two o'clock in the morning, when we'd walk the beach home to South Cape May.

THE WAR COMES TO CAPE MAY

Another thing that affected us greatly—all of us—was World War II. It altered our lives tremendously. From 1940 onward, my brothers, my friends and I were all preparing to go into the service in some way, knowing full well that the war was not going to end anytime soon. Overall, there was a lot of activity in the Cape May area involving the military, both in the water and on land.

Officially, the United States declared war in December 1941. In Cape May, the Coast Guard began patrolling the beaches immediately. In the summer of '42, there were two armed guards walking the beach every four hours, around the clock. They ordered a strict blackout past eight o'clock at night, for fear that even house lamps would leave enough light for German submarines to spot ships offshore.

The German U-boats had a distinct presence off the Jersey shore, and right near Cape May, specifically. The Cape May area was very sensitive, because the Delaware Bay is the third largest port in the country, and a good deal of traffic to and from the Philadelphia Navy Yard came through the bay. A large navy destroyer, the *Jacob Jones*, was sunk by a German submarine in February 1942, just off the coast of Cape May, and only eleven men survived. Our ships destroyed some of the submarines, too. The remains of a number of sunken tankers are still found there, deep at the bottom of the ocean. In 1945, right after the German surrender in Europe, a U-boat surfaced about forty miles off the coast, gave itself up and was escorted in by the USS *Pillsbury*.[53]

The communities on shore were all ordered to be very careful with lighting, and we had to hang black pull-down shades on all our windows. But one night, during the time I was working at the bowling alley, I came home, as usual, about two o'clock in the morning. I went up to my room on the second floor and, without thinking, I pulled the cord on the light fixture that hung from the ceiling lamp—just a plain bulb in its socket. The shade wasn't down, and my window faced right out on the ocean. The light bulb started swinging and blinking. I pulled the shade down. It didn't catch at first. It bounced back up, and then I pulled it down again.

It seemed about two seconds later that there was a banging on the front door. My mother was sleeping downstairs. She got up and saw the Coast Guard pull open the house door. They cocked their guns and asked, "Who is signaling on the second floor?" She had no idea what was going on. I came down to see what the racket was, and the Coast Guard started interrogating me. I said, shaking, "I just got home from work at the bowling alley! I forgot to pull the shades down before I turned on the light!" They still had their guns pointed at me and commanded me back upstairs, telling me to reenact the whole thing. They finally believed me and left, but it took me a long time to fall asleep that night. From then on, the first thing I did when I got in my room at night was to pull down the window shade in my room.

Also in the summer of 1942, right near us, close to the South Cape May borough line, the Army Corps of Engineers built a huge bunker on the beach, Battery 223, the ruins of which are still there today. It was built of reinforced concrete with a roof and walls six feet thick, part of a coastal defense system along the Atlantic. A similar one sat across the bay, in Lewes, Delaware, so that the entire area was guarded. The bunker had round turrets with six-inch guns on either side, which were actually installed first, in the summer of 1941, before the bunker was built, and there were another four coast-artillery guns in front. Originally, the bunker was nine hundred feet inland, the top of it covered with sod as camouflage. It looked like a hill of grass, a big lawn, with two squares jutting out into the sea. The bunker itself was not visible. The whole installation was a substation of Fort Miles, in Delaware, which, at the time, was the second largest coastal fortification in the United States. As part of this, even closer to South Cape May, there

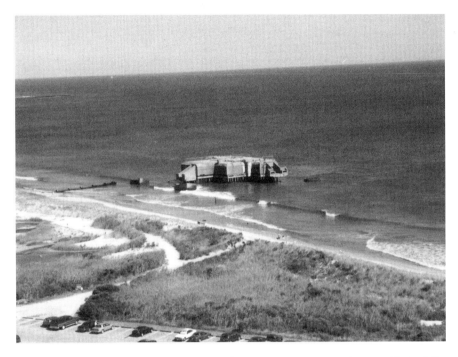

U.S. Army bunker ruins seen from Cape May Point Lighthouse, 1995. *Courtesy of Robert W. Elwell Sr.*

was another installation, with four ninety-millimeter artillery guns that had a large firing range—more than ten miles, practically the entire distance across the bay to Delaware.[54]

These fortifications were all fenced off and patrolled constantly, not really visible even to the people in our little borough, although my brother Vincent remembers wandering up there and seeing the huge guns from the end of the South Cape May beach. A platoon of soldiers was stationed there, with barracks on the site today of a parking lot for the Cape May Point State Park. After the war, the guns were removed and the navy took over the bunker, installing a radar station there until the early 1960s. With all of the erosion at the beach, the entire concrete bunker has long been completely exposed.

By 1943, my days in the thriving borough of South Cape May were over. Knowing I'd be drafted, I joined the navy. I did most of my tour of duty in Hawaii—a great bit of luck, considering how much I loved those summers in South Cape May. By the time I came back from the war, South Cape May had become a very different place.

CHAPTER 7

Storming and Vanishing

THE GREAT ATLANTIC HURRICANE OF 1944

I was still in the navy when the biggest storm ever hit Cape May, the Great Atlantic Hurricane of September 14, 1944, with winds of more than ninety miles an hour. My family wrote to me about it: "It's leveled South Cape May," they said. A few houses were left standing, and they stayed up for a few more years, but that storm pretty much knocked everything out. It hit the entire Northeast coast, from North Carolina to Maine, and according to the U.S. Weather Bureau, destroyed nearly one thousand homes, half of them in New Jersey.

The *Cape May Star and Wave* called that 1944 hurricane the worst storm in Cape May's history, describing how the city emerged "with its boardwalk completely destroyed, Convention Hall wrecked, virtually every beachfront cottage and hotel damaged by the impact of storm-tossed wreckage and mountainous waves, and the majority of homes and buildings throughout the city damaged to some extent by either wind or water." A tidal wave built up offshore, while the wind suddenly shifted from northeast to northwest about five o'clock that Thursday afternoon, and then "the full force of the mass of water was unleashed against the beach," with most of the damage sustained in a matter of minutes.[55]

In the aftermath, South Cape May and the meadows were absolutely flooded with water—it went all the way up to Sunset Boulevard, several feet deep in one section of the road, causing Cape May Point to be marooned for hours. Seven months after the hurricane, on April 30, 1945, the borough of South Cape May officially ceased to exist, and the land became part of Lower Township.[56]

By the time of the storm, my father had been borough clerk for a few years. In a tremendous stroke of luck, he had sold the bigger house on Ninth Avenue—what used to be Aunt Jennie's place—a year before the hurricane hit, taking the house down with it. It was not that he had a crystal ball; he and my mother were simply very frugal. By that time, they had just a few children still living at home. Trese was in nursing school, and Walt and Dick were getting ready to go into the service. Aside from them, it was just Rita, Paul and Vincent. My parents figured it didn't make any sense to maintain the bigger house with the family growing smaller. They sold it easily enough—I think they got $6,000 for it—and moved into my grandfather's old cottage on Eighth near Mount Vernon Avenue. My father had inherited that little place, and for years after my grandmother's death in 1938, he had been renting it out or letting other members of the family stay there. When I got back from the navy, that small cottage was the summer home base for the family, and I only stayed there for short bits of time.

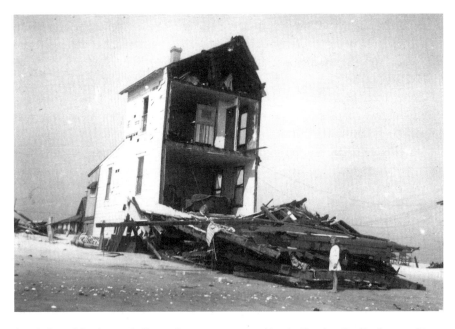

South Cape May house similar to the one once owned by the Burcher family, destroyed in a storm. *Courtesy of Cape May County Historical and Genealogical Society.*

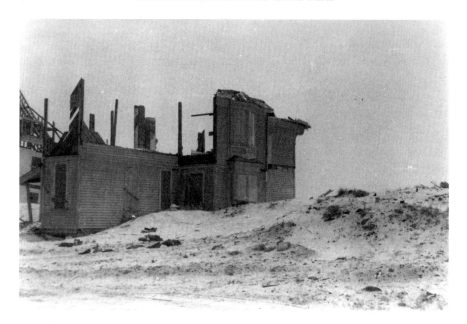

South Cape May house similar to the Burcher family home. *Courtesy of Cape May County Historical and Genealogical Society.*

Even though I wasn't anywhere near the area for the hurricane, I certainly heard all about it. My brother Vincent was nine years old at the time, and he remembers being at our home in Berlin the day it came. The eye of the hurricane went right over our house, and standing there, he could see the clouds swirling around. Very shortly afterward, he drove down with my parents to see what was left of South Cape May. They were all happy to see that the small cottage, which was set back a few hundred yards from the beach, was pretty much undisturbed, although you could see the watermark on the walls.

But elsewhere in the borough, there was debris all over. Roofs had been pulled off houses and were now piled up in the meadows. The houses were all wood-framed, and there was wood all over the place. The water level was very high, flooding the area. Vincent grabbed two fallen telephone poles and some other lumber lying around and built a raft to float around the area with a pole—like Huck Finn or Tom Sawyer—looking at all the debris. He remembers getting bored with this after a while, and then our brother Ed, who was thirty-one at the time, asked if he could borrow it. Some hours later, there was Ed, pulling the raft with a rope. He had picked up all the lumber and windows that he could salvage to use for his own cottage, including a large cupboard he found in the marsh—it took up a whole wall inside his place.

Storms in the 1930s and the Source of Erosion

The first storm I recall experiencing in South Cape May was when I was less than ten years old. I remember the water coming down the streets, and we children thought it was glorious. We built up little sand dunes just for fun to try to stop the water. The water didn't come into that bigger house of ours, though, because the house was highly elevated.

I have a more vivid recollection of the nor'easter on September 18, 1936, when I was thirteen. My brother Jim and I borrowed (commandeered, really) a canoe from the garage in one of the houses, and we paddled all the way from our house in South Cape May to the end of Cape May Point at Sunset Beach, and back, with two or three feet of water underneath the canoe.

That was the first major inundation I saw, where the water covered Mount Vernon Avenue and came right up to my grandfather's doorstep. Our house on Ninth Avenue didn't have a water problem at the time. Some of my brothers carried my grandmother out during the hurricane, and we all gathered at the Kellys' house, which was set back from the ocean, past Mount Vernon toward Sunset Boulevard. The storm was raging, but we all assumed that the Kellys' house would be safe, because it was high up and very strongly built. It obviously was, since it still survives today. But for all we knew, that house could have blown down, too.

Like Vincent with that later hurricane, I have a very vivid recollection of the eye of the storm. It was absolutely impressive, looking up to see the beautiful sky. In the next hour and a half, the raging seas came in over the streets. That was the beginning of the end of South Cape May. The hurricane knocked down a number of houses, and that's when people started abandoning efforts to try to save anything.

South Cape May was mentioned prominently in the newspaper when that 1936 nor'easter hit. The beachfront house of Harvey Mentzer, the mayor of South Cape May at the time, was completely destroyed, and the *Cape May Star and Wave* placed a picture of the wreck on the front page. Other residents' houses were demolished by the storm as well. Headlines described an eighty-mile-an-hour gale and "mountainous seas" raking the beachfront. "South Cape May bore the brunt of the storm damage."[57] More than twenty South Cape May residents were removed from their homes by the Coast Guard. Out at sea, seven members of a fishing crew on a large steamer drowned at the height of the storm.

It's an odd coincidence that Harvey Mentzer's house was destroyed, considering all the work he did with the borough council in the years leading

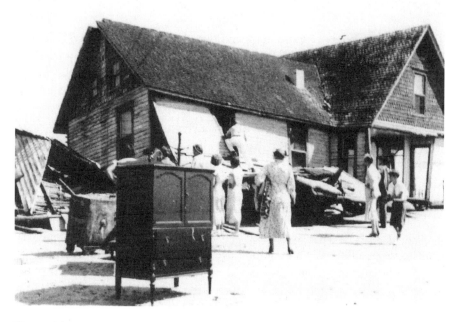

Home of South Cape May mayor Harvey Mentzer, destroyed in 1936 nor'easter. *Courtesy of Cape May County Historical and Genealogical Society.*

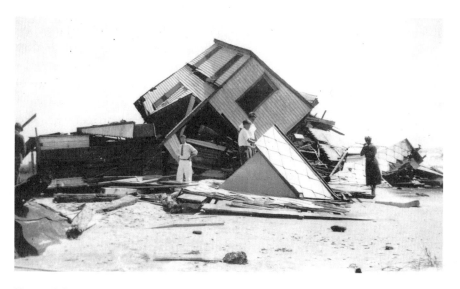

Home of Oswald Milligan, September 1936. *Courtesy of Robert W. Elwell Sr.*

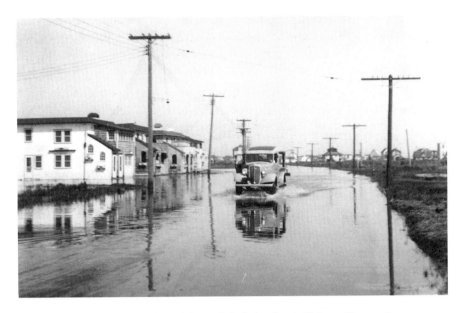

The Spanish Villas of South Cape May on left, facing flooded Mount Vernon Avenue. *Courtesy of Cape May County Historical and Genealogical Society.*

up to that 1936 storm. The council minutes note that Mentzer was planning a trip to Washington on behalf of the borough in January 1935 to attend a "Beach Protection Meeting." Efforts by Mentzer and the council on the issue dated back to at least 1933, including working with engineer Morgan Hand to develop a shore protection program and applying for a grant from the Federal Emergency Administration of Public Works. The plan called for "a copper bearing steel sheet pile bulkhead together with a series of jetties of the same material, every other one having rock treatment." They researched historic maps, charting the shifting high-water lines of South Cape May back to 1842, and the council passed a resolution on November 7, 1933, noting that "it is conceded by all authorities" that any shore protection along the coast on the peninsula that excluded South Cape May would work direct hardships on the borough. They attributed the damage done to the shoreline to the Cape May Inlet jetties, at Cape May's easternmost point abutting Wildwood Crest, first built by the Army Corps of Engineers in 1913.[58]

Recent studies also point to the Cape May Inlet jetties as the cause of major changes in the beaches in Cape May City, South Cape May and Cape May Point. Especially notable is Norbert Psuty and Douglas D. Ofiara's work at the Rutgers Institute of Marine and Coastal Sciences for the New Jersey

Department of Environmental Protection. Psuty and Ofiara identify the series of groins, or smaller jetties, set along the Cape May City beach, which were all in place by the early 1930s, as responsible for the severely receded shoreline in South Cape May. The last groin in that series is just west of Second Avenue, set where Third Avenue would have been if it had been developed.[59]

THE 1950 STORM

After the 1944 hurricane, there were other sizable storms. Damage from the November 25, 1950 storm actually exceeded that of the hurricane of 1944. The *Star and Wave* reported on an eighty-eight-mile-an-hour gale and "giant waves, whipped into fury by an easterly wind that reached full-hurricane proportions [which] flooded most of the city and drove hundreds of local residents from their homes." Cape May Point was completely isolated, with Sunset Boulevard covered by water, and "in South Cape May, where erosion has taken tremendous tolls through the years, several houses were threatened by the pouring of the waves. One tilted precariously but remained standing, and in the meadows behind the tiny community several small cottages were wrecked by the flood."[60]

Among those small cottages were Ed and Dot Burcher's place and my grandfather's old house. Shortly thereafter, Ed bought lots on Sunset Boulevard from John Rutherford—former farmland—and the two houses were moved there. Dot remembers the storm coming in and their house moving right out to sea, floating like a box. And just as quickly, it came back in with the surge of the tide and sank in the mud of the meadow. To top things off, people came around looting after the storm, going right inside the house and taking the crib, an ironing board, the icebox, anything they could get hold of. It was one thing for Ed to salvage some lumber and other material out of the marsh—this was something else altogether.

The Kellys' house, next door to mine on Sunset Boulevard now, was moved not long afterward, too, as was the house that belonged to Mary Black and her family—I don't remember her husband's name—which now has a sign in front of it calling it the "Cape Betty Mae." Also moved about that time was the home of the Keans, joining our old neighbors, the Watsons, on South Broadway in Cape May City.

The old Rutschman house—the house the *Star and Wave* said "tilted precariously"—was out in the meadows until the very end, up to 1954, according to some accounts. Badly deteriorated, its first floor was virtually gone; all that was left were the posts that held up the second and third floors.

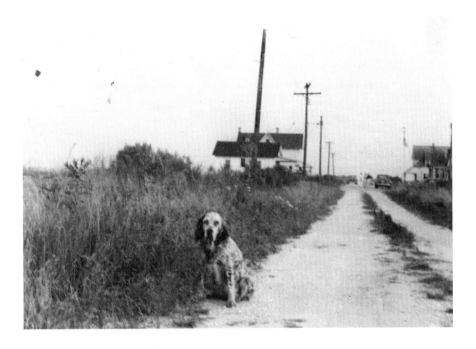

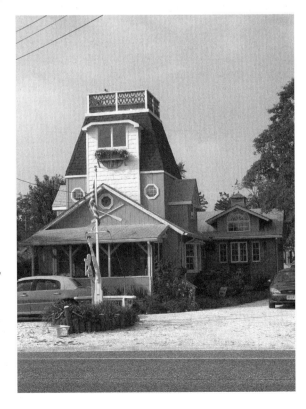

Above: View of Eighth Avenue in South Cape May, showing the home of Mary Black and family near center, past pole, 1949. *Author's collection.*

Right: Former home of Mary Black and family on Sunset Boulevard, 2006. The tower was added after its move from South Cape May. *Photo by Robert Kenselaar.*

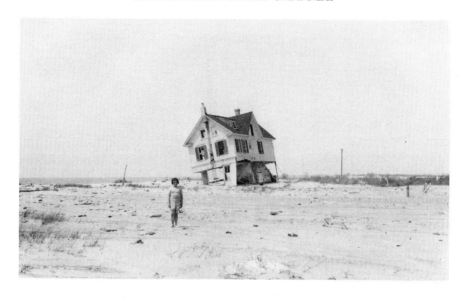

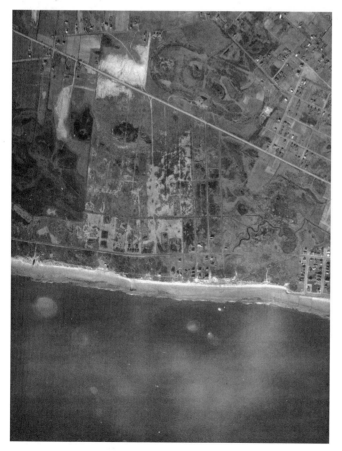

Above: Former Rutschman house in the meadows, August 1951. *Photo by Isaac B. Zwalley. Courtesy of H. Gerald MacDonald.*

Left and next two pages: Aerial views of South Cape May. 1933 at left. *Nationwide Environmental Title Research, LLC.*

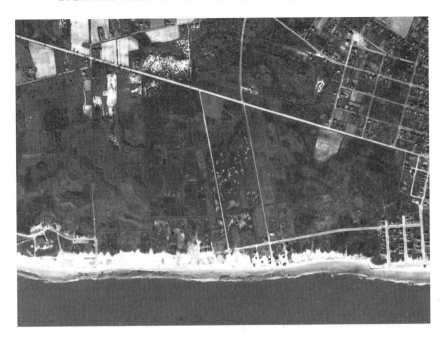

1944.

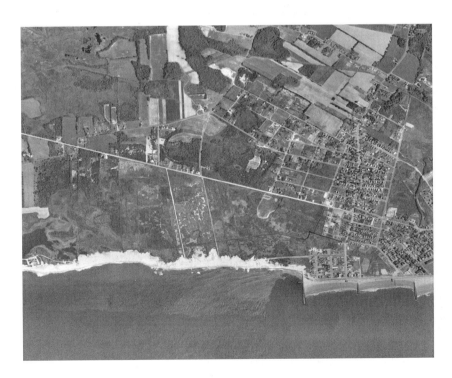

1956.

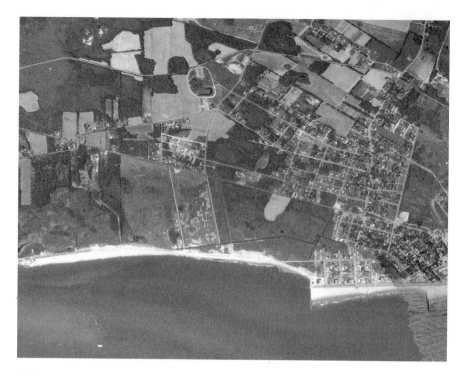

1970.

If it did, in fact, remain there until 1954, it would have survived two other large storms, a nor'easter in 1953 and Hurricane Carol on August 31, 1954, although that one just "skirted" Cape May.[61]

There were a few house-moving businesses in the area in those days. Billy Snyder, with whom I caddied when we were boys, owned one of them. He moved the Kellys' house, my parents' and my brother Ed's. From what I heard, moving the Kellys' house actually killed him. In the process of moving it, the culverts weren't strong enough to hold it, and the house fell in the creek. It took a long time for him to finish that job, in bad weather. He came down with pneumonia, and not long after he moved the house, he died.

My family's two small cottages, the Rutschmans' and the Kellys' houses were set back a little ways from the ocean, so it naturally followed that they would be among the survivors left in South Cape May. The houses close to the ocean were a different story. There was barely anything to protect them at all. One large dune covered with sea grass acted somewhat as a barrier. But without any of the beach protection Harvey Mentzer was lobbying for back in the 1930s, nothing was going to stop that ocean from coming in.

CHAPTER 8

Sunset Boulevard,
Cattle and Birds

MY OWN COTTAGE

By the mid-1950s, there was nothing much left of the borough of South Cape May in its original location but the bits and pieces of abandoned properties still in the meadow or at the bottom of the sea. We used to see parts of the buildings well into the 1960s—boards, bricks from chimneys, pipes and even toilets.

The cluster of homes moved to Sunset Boulevard in West Cape May—including my parents' and my brother Ed's cottages—sat just on the other side of the old borough line, all close to one another. Before long, various other members of my family were staking out on Sunset Boulevard, with my brother Paul and my sisters Claire and Trese all settling there. Eventually, nieces, in-laws and extended family followed, to the point where some of the locals called the neighborhood Burcherville.

You might think it was my strong family ties and the magic of the legacy of South Cape May that drew me to build my own little cottage on Sunset Boulevard, overlooking the site of the old borough. But it was really just a mix of impulse, accident and pure luck.

I was still in college at that time, having switched from Drexel, where I enrolled before joining the navy, to Temple University, changing my major from engineering to teaching. Vida Santosuosso and I were married in 1948.

I had written to my South Cape May girlfriend, Marie Megenedy, all through the war, but as soon as I saw Vida when I came home, I knew she was the girl I would marry. We had two children by 1952, Joanne and Mary. In earlier years, I had worked summer student-teaching jobs, but Vida wanted to spend the summer at the shore, so I looked into working there. Abbott's Dairy in Wildwood was hiring, and I took a job delivering milk. Then I had to find us a place to live. Abbott's gave me some leads on apartments, but the rent was going to take every penny of what I'd make as a milkman.

I looked into buying a lot of my own, thinking I'd build my own cottage on it, as my brother Ed had done. I investigated Wildwood Crest and Cape May City to see if it had any cheap, city-owned lots, but without luck. So I checked on West Cape May, going over to the West Side Market on Broadway to see Charlie Douglas, the owner, who also happened to be the borough clerk. He had one lot available—the last one—on Sunset Boulevard, right next to my brother Paul's. I gave Charlie ten dollars to hold it and told him I'd be back the next week with the rest of the money. I went over to look at the lot, and it wasn't much to see—some brush, stagnant water and one little high spot.

I borrowed money from my father-in-law to pay Charlie. Later that week, I stumbled on an ad in *McCall's* magazine. "You can build your summer house for five hundred dollars," it said. The plans cost one dollar. I sent away for them, but they weren't much help. I had no clue how to get started, but I figured it made sense to dig a trench to lay the foundation. I called a man in to pour the concrete the next Saturday. He gave me some advice, but in the end, it was three inches higher on one end than the other. Close enough, I thought.

I was living at my parents' cottage and started building the frame in the wee hours of the morning before I went to deliver milk. I'd come home at night and have Ed or Paul help me, joined by some college friends on weekends.

I found out the hard way how difficult it is to build a house that's even reasonably square. Your measurements really have to be exact. It drove me crazy. It was June 17, 1952. I'll never forget it. There were two critical measurements, diagonally across the square from both sides, and I just couldn't get them to match. The heat was unbearable, but the worst of it was the gnats. They were so distracting, I put on a heavy rain slicker to try to keep them off. At one point, I was so frustrated that I found myself taking a hammer and literally hitting myself on the head with it. It was about 8:30 at night. I ran from my lot down to the South Cape May beach and just flopped in the ocean. I woke up the next morning, not knowing where I was

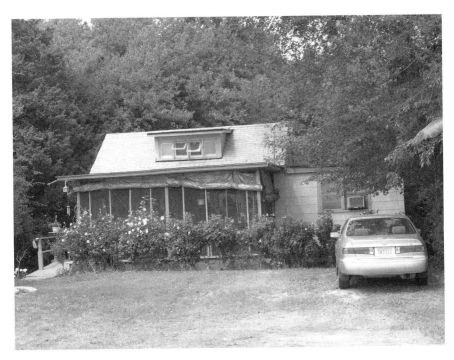

Cottage of Joseph Burcher and family on Sunset Boulevard. *Photo by Robert Kenselaar.*

or how I got there, until I looked up and found myself lying on the beach, covered in sand.

I finally got the frame square and anchored it in. In another month, the siding and roof were up, windows were in and I had crates set up for steps. I drove in a well, another thing that nearly killed me, working nonstop from eight o'clock in the morning until eight o'clock at night, pounding the ground. Over the years, our family kept growing; first Bonnie, and then Christopher and Amy were born. I added two bedrooms and a back porch onto the original cottage. Like my brother Ed, I used furniture, wood and other pieces of old homes from South Cape May that I found in the meadows here and there.

THE COW PASTURE

I put in a good-sized picture window in the front of the cottage, looking out on Sunset Boulevard and the meadows where South Cape May once stood.

For years, when the children were small, aside from the sky and the dune on the horizon, there was also a herd of cattle out there. A local farmer, Les Rea, put eighty cows in the meadows, along with one mean bull. He had no barn; he just fenced the area off and kept them out in the open until well into the 1970s. The children used to go up to them at the fence to try to feed them, and every once in a while, one would break through and wander onto Sunset Boulevard. They were Black Angus, raised for beef.

The Rea farm was spread out over into West Cape May, west of Second Avenue, with a stand selling fresh corn and tomatoes on Bayshore Road. That farm had been in Les's family for many years, and as children, we used to walk from our house on the beach in South Cape May to his stand for fresh vegetables. Lima beans were his biggest crop for a long time. One of the big frozen food producers contracted with him, and he grew hundreds of acres of them. Les would bring tons of lima bean residue in to feed the cows, which made for a strong odor on Sunset Boulevard until he started leaving it closer to the beach.

One summer night, some of his cattle were stolen. Les came to my cottage, knocked on the door and asked me, "Joe, did you hear any rustlers out there, any cattle trucks or anything? Because somebody stole thirteen of my cattle! Young heifers!"

The land was all basically flat when the cattle were there—no brush or trees, mainly grass. There was a pond, but not a big one, nothing like the series of ponds that are there now. There was usually a lot of what I'd call brown muck, though. The cattle would either drink from it or Les would drain it. One souvenir I have from those days—which I display for my students in the classroom—is a skull that I found from a cow that died out there in the meadows, which I don't think Les knew about. There was one other feature on the edge of what was the pasture at Sunset Boulevard: an ice cream stand that sat on what is now the parking lot for the Nature Conservancy preserve.

Ultimately, Les worked out an arrangement with the State of New Jersey so that the Rea farm was designated as a protected area. It's still a working farm, and as I understand it, it's going to continue either as a working farm or as a protected area indefinitely. There are some large, rusty old weathered pieces of farm equipment on some parts of the land, and I understand most of that will simply stay there, deteriorating slowly. It's all quite picturesque, actually.

The arrangement made between the Rea farm and the state was a recent development, within the last several years. The cow pasture itself ended some twenty years ago, when the Nature Conservancy took over the land.

The Meadows

In the period before the Nature Conservancy became involved with the South Cape May Meadows, the entire Cape May area was increasingly turning into a mecca for bird-watchers and naturalists, a trend that was part of a long tradition in ornithological circles. The history dates back to the eighteenth century and Alexander Wilson—considered the most prominent American ornithologist before Audubon—who explored the Cape May County area. Witmer Stone, another especially notable figure, served as the director of the Academy of Natural Sciences in Philadelphia, among other positions. Stone summered in Cape May every year from 1916 until he died in 1939, and his *Bird Studies at Old Cape May* includes many references to South Cape May in addition to the passages quoted in the beginning of this book. Ernest A. Choate, author of the standard reference *Dictionary of American Bird Names*, followed in Stone's footsteps. Choate was a resident of South Cape May in the 1930s before moving to Cape May Point. He served as principal of Germantown High School in Philadelphia for many years and joined the Delaware Valley Ornithological Club in 1932, serving briefly as president. (Stone was a founding member.) The 1965 edition of Stone's *Bird Studies* includes an updated list of species recorded in Cape May that was compiled by Choate and includes the glossy ibis he sighted in South Cape May in 1953. Choate and his wife, along with Mayor Harvey Mentzer, were among the South Cape May residents temporarily relocated from their homes when the 1936 nor'easter hit.[62]

Another ornithologist who has been active in Cape May in recent years is Pete Dunne, who's written a number of books, contributes regularly to the major birding publications and is vice-president of the New Jersey Audubon Society. The Cape May Bird Observatory, of which he's director, was founded in 1975. His first major work was a study of hawks in the area, and his knowledge of Cape May bird species is encyclopedic. One of his early books, *Tales of a Low-Rent Birder*, is a collection of essays he wrote in the 1970s and '80s, all tied to Cape May. I used to see him once in a while, out in the meadows during his early days in the area, in the wee morning hours.

Pete Dunne was actively involved in establishing the South Cape May Meadows as a Nature Conservancy preserve in 1981. A firm named Combustion Engineering owned the land, and there were plans by developers to turn it into either condominiums or an "environmental campground." The Nature Conservancy had a mechanism in place to purchase land that was a habitat for endangered species, such as some of the birds that frequented

South Cape May. Pete and his colleagues contacted the conservancy, and Bud Cook, director of the Pennsylvania and New Jersey chapter at the time, spearheaded the purchase of the Meadows, more than two hundred acres.[63]

The Nature Conservancy has done a tremendous amount of work over the last several years to restore the area, working with the Army Corps of Engineers and the New Jersey Department of Environmental Protection. The shoreline, which had eroded greatly, has been restored somewhat, with tons of sand pumped in, and the dune has been built up considerably to hold the sea back. The main trails—what were once Ninth and Twelfth Avenues—have been raised. Millions of dollars have been invested in the restoration of the area overall.

The Meadows today are filled with a mixed and wide variety of wildflowers and grasses: wood sorrel, yellow thistle, swamp rose, sumac, goldenrod, beach plums and bayberry, as well as phragmites, of course, the invasive reeds that are difficult to control, although the Nature Conservancy has done a good job of keeping them down. Birds that are especially common include swallows, egrets, herons, geese, swans and hawks, as well as little sandpipers along the ocean, past the dunes. Not as visible, but still somewhat prevalent, are the four-legged creatures: muskrats, weasels and frogs, along with occasional snapping turtles. Butterflies—especially monarchs—and hummingbirds are common, too, and you'll also see snakes from time to time. There are several ponds in the meadow, with a mix of fresh and salt water, fed by the ocean spilling past the dunes during heavy storms and by the fresh-water Cape Island Creek, which we used to call the Deepee and which formed the border of South Cape May and Cape May City. That creek continues to run underground through the woodland to Swain's Hardware and ultimately Delaware Bay.

What the refuge is probably most noted for, though, are two endangered species of small migratory birds: piping plovers and least terns. They aren't actually in the meadow itself; they're found just past the dune, closer to the ocean. The conservancy has fenced off a large area there to protect the birds' nesting spots, and they also place cages over some of the piping plover nests within the area.

Piping plovers are round-headed, with stubby beaks and thick necks, sandy-colored with some black rings, and they make a soft, whistled "peep" sound. I've seen them described as six or seven inches long, but they seem smaller to me, although I may be thinking of the chicks. Least terns are seven or eight inches long, with longer heads and black-tipped yellow beaks, pale gray and white, with white heads and black caps, and they have a somewhat

From the 1920s to the Present: A Firsthand Account

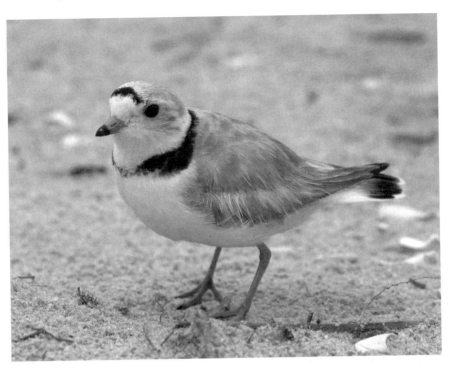

Piping plover in South Cape May Meadows. *©DamonNoe/The Nature Conservancy.*

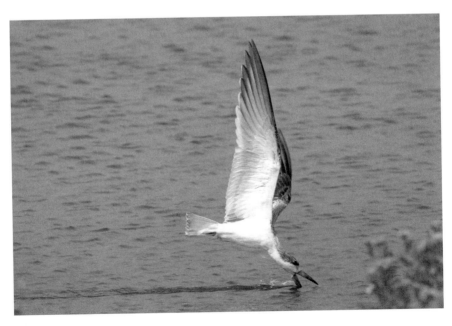

Immature black skimmer in South Cape May Meadows. *©DamonNoe.*

louder, longer call. The terns have fared better than the plovers in general, because they're communal nesters that do a good job of defending their turf by dive-bombing on threats to their community.[64]

Both the plovers and the terns were common along the Atlantic coast in the nineteenth century, but they nearly disappeared because they became popular in the millinery trade. Pete Dunne remembers seeing a piping plover on one of his grandmother's hats. They were protected by the Migratory Bird Treaty Act in the early twentieth century, but increasing development and the growing recreational use of beaches made it difficult for them to thrive.

Not to take away from the work the Nature Conservancy has done, but I'd say that all in all, including the ponds, the birds, the animals, the brush and the other vegetation, the area today is quite similar to the way it was back when I was a boy. I'm sure I'd get an argument from many—especially Witmer Stone, if he were still alive. In my day, there weren't many houses there. It was mostly one big meadow, almost a swamp, really. The houses that were left in South Cape May were mainly up by the beach, a good four hundred yards from the boulevard. We'd see swallows out in the meadows, feeding on all the mosquitoes, and the hummingbirds that came in to feed on the milkweed. Just like today, there were so many birds out there, especially in late August, September and October.

Closing Note

If you walked all the way through the South Cape May Meadows today down the path that was once Ninth Avenue and you stood on top of the big sand dune near the ocean, you'd be near where Mount Vernon Avenue was when I was a boy. You'd be near it, but shifted in a little bit—the area where the road ran and where most of the old houses were is now actually under water. Mount Vernon was just a two-lane road, of course, not as wide as the dune is now. It ran straight from Cape May City through South Cape May down to Cape May Point. Today, if you look east, on the left toward the city from the dune, you can see the small bit of Mount Vernon Avenue that remains, just three blocks long, dead-ending abruptly into the sand. You can also see the tower of the Catholic church, Our Lady Star of the Sea, where I sold newspapers after Sunday mass, and south of that, you can make out the towers of those distinctive homes designed by Stephen Decatur Button, moved away from the Mount Vernon beachfront before my time. And if you turn around, due north, you can see the Kellys' old gray house on Sunset Boulevard, with the roof of my cottage peeking out to the left of it and the old Rutschman house, now painted pink, on the corner to the right.

When I think back on the confluence of factors that brought my family and me to South Cape May, I marvel at how fortunate we all were. So many great times and great memories. I think just a little, too, of what might have been. What if my great-grandfather, John Burcher, had stayed in Bermuda?

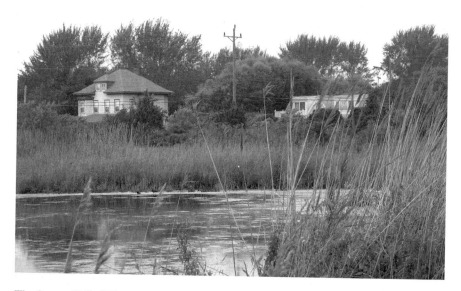

The former Kelly/Wilson and Rutschman houses, as seen from Ninth Avenue trail in South Cape May Meadows, 2006. *Photo by Robert Kenselaar.*

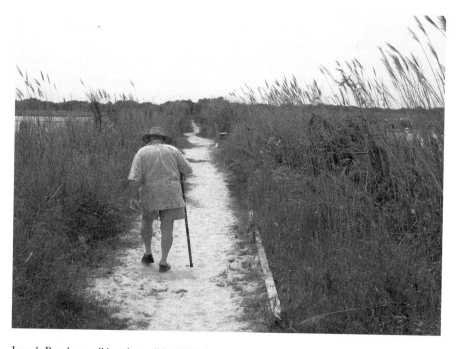

Joseph Burcher walking the trail in 2006 that was once Ninth Avenue and led to his family's South Cape May home. *Photo by Robert Kenselaar.*

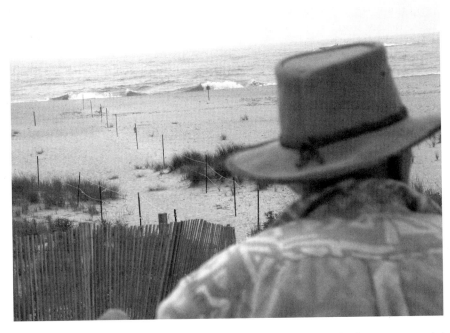

Joseph Burcher, looking at the ocean where his family's South Cape May home once stood. *Photo by Robert Kenselaar.*

What if my great-aunt Jennie paid off that mortgage for $1,000 and held onto her wonderful home in South Cape May? What if that last storm in 1950 had blown out to sea instead of knocking around the two cottages of my brother Ed and my parents? And what if high tide had come in that summer night in 1952, when I collapsed and fell into a deep sleep on the old South Cape May beach after nearly losing my mind in the heat while trying to build a house on my own?

I also wonder about the fate of South Cape May and the meadows I can look out on now, if things had developed a little differently. Back in 1899, there were those efforts I mentioned early in the book to consolidate Cape May City and the boroughs of Cape May Point, West Cape May and South Cape May and to build sea walls to protect their combined eight miles of beachfront. Had those things happened, land in South Cape May would have been much more secure—and much more expensive by the 1920s. My family might not have come looking for property there at all. The stately homes of John Lonabaugh, Peter Day, Samuel Bailie and others would still be standing there, facing the ocean, right on the beach. The Rutschman and Kelly houses and the New Mount Vernon Hotel would still be alongside them, fully intact.

By today, hundreds of other summer homes would also be there. There would be a mix of Victorians, Cape Cods and maybe here and there an odd A frame, as we see at the Point. Instead, what we have are wildflowers, bullfrogs, hummingbirds, egrets and piping plovers. And for me, plenty of memories, too.

Notes

ABBREVIATIONS:

PI: *Philadelphia Inquirer*
SoC: *Star of the Cape*
S&W: *Cape May Star and Wave*

CHAPTER 1

1. Witmer Stone, *Bird Studies at Old Cape May: An Ornithology of Coastal New Jersey* (Philadelphia: Delaware Valley Ornithological Club, 1937), 15, 30.
2. *S&W*, March 13, 1926.
3. Major sources for this section include: Jeffrey M. Dorwart, *Cape May County, New Jersey: The Making of and American Resort Community* (New Brunswick, NJ: Rutgers University Press, 1992); Maurice Beesley, *Sketch of the Early History of Cape May County* (Trenton, NJ: True American, 1857); Edward S. Wheeler, *Scheyichbi and the Strand, or, Early Days along the Delaware* (Philadelphia: J.B. Lippincott, 1876); Herbert M. Beitel and Vance C. Enck, *Cape May County: A Pictorial History* (Norfolk, VA: Donning Company, 1988); and Joan Berkey, *Early Architecture of Cape May County, New Jersey: The Heavy Timber Frame Legacy* (Cape May Court

House, NJ: Cape May County Historical and Genealogical Society, 2008).

4. *Map of Mark Devine Property, Cape May, N.J.*, as surveyed by E.P. Taylor and Son, 1885. No. 257 in Archives of the Cape May County Clerk. Shows property of Mark Devine and previous owners.

5. *Philadelphia Public Ledger*, July 7, 1841.

6. Robert Crozer Alexander, *Ho! For Cape Island* (Philadelphia: Edward Stern & Company, 1956), 121–30; *Trenton State Gazette*, July 13, 1853; *Illustrated London News*, September 17, 1853; *Philadelphia Public Ledger*, September 8, 1856; *Philadelphia Evening Bulletin*, September 8, 1856; *PI*, April 14, 1888.

7. John H. Campbell, *History of the Friendly Sons of St. Patrick* (Philadelphia: Hibernian Society, 1892), 390.

8. *PI*, May 11, 1882.

9. A major source of information in this section is Robert C. Alexander, "Light of Asia," *Cape May County Magazine of History and Genealogy* 9 (1990): 288–92. See also Joe J. Jordan, *Cape May Point: The Illustrated History: 1875 to the Present* (Atglen, PA: Schiffer Publishing, 2003).

CHAPTER 2

10. George E. Thomas and Carl E. Doebley, *Cape May: Queen of the Seaside Resorts: Its History and Architecture* (Cape May, NJ: Knossus Project, Mid-Atlantic Center for the Arts, 1998), 56. Other detail on Button in this section also draws from this source.

11. Building contracts for the Lonabaugh, et al., and Day houses designed by Button are in the collections of the Athenaeum of Philadelphia.

12. *SoC*, March 23, 1888, April 13, 1888, August 3, 1888.

13. Richard J. Webster, "Stephen D. Button: Italianate Stylist" (master's thesis, University of Delaware, 1963).

14. James Fergusson, *The Illustrated Handbook of Architecture* (London: John Murray, 1855), 789–90.

15. *SoC*, October 24, 1903, November 7, 1903, December 19, 1903.

16. Details on South Cape May families and homes included in this section compiled in part from U.S. Census records accessed 2006–2010 through http://www.ancestry.com. Other information drawn from news articles, including: Lonabaugh: *PI*, November 1, 1896. Day: *PI*, March 17, 1904. Wilbraham: *S&W*, August 26, 1922. Rutschman: *The Pennsylvanian*, March 3, 1911.

17. Sanborn-Perris Map Company, *Insurance Maps of the New Jersey Coast*, vol. 4, Cape May County (New York: Sanborn-Perris Map Co., Ltd., 1890; annotated [1902–3]). Later maps consulted: Sanborn Map Company, *Insurance Maps of the New Jersey Coast*, vol. 4 (Cape May County, NY: Sanborn Map Co., 1909, 1929, 1935, 1949). Re: incorporation, see typescript transcription by Cape May County Library Commission, in Cape May Court House County Library clipping file.

18. Emil R. Salvini, *The Summer City by the Sea: Cape May, New Jersey: An Illustrated History* (New Brunswick, NJ: Rutgers University Press, 2004), 68; *PI*, March 5, 1896, September 19, 1904, May 20, 1908, March 4, 1922.

19. *S&W*, July 4, 1985; interviews with Eleanor Graham Foster and Don Foster.

Chapter 3

20. Thomas and Doebley, *Cape May*, 66–67. Williams's obituary, *Cape May Wave*, April 20, 1895.

21. *Cape May Wave*, February 16, 1884.

22. Building contracts for the New Mount Vernon Hotel and Rutschman residence, Athenaeum of Philadelphia.

23. Building contract for the Miller residence provided by Miriam Pedrick. Congregation Rodeph Shalom, *Annual* 25 (1917–18), 53; *The History of Rodeph Shalom Congregation* (Philadelphia, 1926), 152–53.

24. *SoC*, July 1, 1892.

25. *SoC*, March 20, 1891, and see note 16, above.

26. Sanborn-Perris Map Co., *Insurance Maps*, vol. 4, 1890, annotated [1902, 1903].

27. *New Jersey County and Municipal Officials* (East Orange, NJ: State Service Bureau, 1929–45); Cape May County Library clipping file; South Cape May, *Borough Council Minutes*.

28. *SoC*, August 19, 1892.

29. New Jersey, Department of State, Census Bureau, *1895 State Census of New Jersey*; *PI*, July 11, 1897; *Trenton Evening Times*, September 11, 1905.

CHAPTER 4

30. *SoC*, July 10, 1891.

31. *SoC*, August 28, 1891.

32. *SoC*, August 15, 1890, February 13, 1891, July 21, 1893, February 13, 1891, July 21, 1893, August 18, 1893.

33. *SoC*, October 20, 1893.

34. *PI*, July 15, 1894, July 23, 1894. The actual official incorporation of South Cape May was in August—election held August 21, petition filed in county clerk's office August 27.

35. *PI*, April 23, 1895, February 26, 1904.

36. *SoC*, November 14, 1890.

37. *SoC*, July 11, 1896, July 10, 1897, July 3, 1897; *PI*, August 5, 1915.

38. *SoC*, January 30, 1891; *PI*, October 13, 1896. General sources: Larry Savadove and Margaret Thomas Buchholz, *Great Storms of the Jersey Shore* (West Creek, NJ: Down the Shore Publishing, 1993); Rick Schwartz, *Hurricanes of the Middle Atlantic States: A Surprising History, from Jamestown to the Present* (Alexandria, VA: Blue Diamond Books, 2007).

39. *PI*, February 3, 1897, October 26, 1897; *Cape May Wave*, October 30, 1897.

40. *PI*, January 14, 1899, March 19, 1900.

41. *PI*, November 25, 1901.

42. *PI*, April 16, 1903.

43. *Cape May Wave*, September 19, 1903.

44. *Cape May Wave*, October 17, 1903; *PI*, October 12, 1903.

45. U.S. Department of Agriculture, Weather Bureau, *Climatological Data for the United States by Sections*, 1918.

46. *S&W*, November 10, 1923, and later weekly issues leading to sale held December 10.

CHAPTER 5

47. Deed, Archives of the Cape May County Clerk.

48. U.S. Census Bureau, *United States Census*, 1860–1930, and other records accessed through http://www.ancestry.com, 2006–2010.

49. Jeffrey M. Dorwart, *The Philadelphia Navy Yard: From the Birth of the U.S. Navy to the Nuclear Age* (Philadelphia: University of Pennsylvania Press, 2001), 147.

50. The house on Eighth Avenue that was directly behind Virginia Gardiner's had the same basic design as hers, and an 1892 building contract at the Philadelphia Athenaeum for that Eighth Avenue house shows its architect was Enos Williams, who contracted with the Mount Vernon Land Company.
51. U.S. Census, 1860–1930, and other records accessed through http://www.ancestry.com, 2006–2010.

CHAPTER 6

52. *S&W*, January 26, 1956; Stone, *Bird Studies at Old Cape May*, 36.
53. *S&W*, May 17, 1945; Salvini, *Summer City by the Sea*, 102.
54. Fort Miles Historical Association, http://www.fortmilesha.org/, U-boat Archive, http://www.uboatarchive.net/, accessed April 2010.

CHAPTER 7

55. *S&W*, September 21, 1944. Other general sources: Savadove and Buchholz, *Great Storms of the Jersey Shore*; Schwartz, *Hurricanes of the Middle Atlantic States.*
56. New Jersey, *Acts of the One Hundred and Sixty-Ninth Legislature of the State of New Jersey: Laws of 1945*, Chapter 267, 799. Approved and effective April 30, 1945. State Senate bill 258, introduced by Redding, March 26, 1945.
57. *S&W*, September 24, 1936.
58. Borough of South Cape May, NJ, *Borough Council Minutes*, November 11, 1933, in volume containing 1927–35, 208.
59. Norbert Psuty and Douglas D. Ofiara, *Coastal Hazard Management: Lessons and Future Directions for New Jersey* (New Brunswick, NJ: Rutgers University Press, 2002), 75–78. The aerial photograph on p. 77 is especially noteworthy.
60. *S&W*, November 30, 1950.
61. *S&W*, September 2, 1954.

CHAPTER 8

62. Ernest A. Choate, *Dictionary of American Bird Names* (Boston: Harvard Common Press, 1985); Witmer Stone, *Bird Studies*, rev. ed. (New York:

Dover Publications, 1965), xiv–xvii; *The Bulletin* [Philadelphia], March 16, 1980; *S&W*, September 24, 1936.

63. Pete Dunne, *Tales of a Low-Rent Birder* (New Brunswick, NJ: Rutgers University Press, 1986); interview with Pete Dunne, December 2009.

64. The Nature Conservancy of New Jersey, William D. and Jane C. Blair Jr., *Cape May Migratory Bird Refuge: Self-Guided Nature Walk* (Delmont, NJ: Nature Conservancy, 1999 [pamphlet]); Clay Sutton and Pat Sutton, *Birds and Birding at Cape May* (Mechanicsburg, PA: Stackpole Books, 2006).

Index

Good Tidings, the 14
grass 14, 74, 83, 86, 98, 102, 104
Great Atlantic Hurricane of 1944
    88–90
Great Depression 71, 72, 73
Greenewald family 45
Greenewald, Jacob 41, 45
Green, Mr. 82, 83
groins 94
Guensheimer family 76, 77
gulls 13

H

Hagan, Edward 26
Hay, Howard 35
Half Moon, the 14
Hand, Morgan 93
Harrison, Benjamin 56
Hartranft, Helen 35
Herzberg family 45
hoboes 73
hotels
  Abbey 25
  Admiral Hotel 81, 82
  Cayman Hotel 39
  Columbia Hotel 28
  Lafayette Hotel 29
  Mount Vernon Hotel 7, 17–19,
      21, 24, 30
  Mount Vernon House 17, 24
  New Mount Vernon Hotel 39,
      40
  South Cape May Hotel 39, 77
  Stockton Hotel 29
  Wilbraham Mansion 35
  Windsor Hotel 29

house moving/relocation 30, 33,
    35, 37, 43, 45, 46, 47, 52, 62,
    94, 98, 99
houses of worship 27, 45, 77
housing stock, total 55
Hoxie, Joseph C. 28
hucksters 57, 82
Hudson, Henry 14
hunting 14, 57, 72
Hurricane Carol 98
hurricanes 88–91, 98. *See also*
    storms

I

icemen 82, 83
Illustrated London News, the 18
immigrants 20, 43, 57, 71
Indians 14, 15, 16
infrastructure 54
Insurance Maps of the New Jersey Coast
    29

J

Jackson Clubhouse 29
Jackson Street 28, 84
Jacob Jones, the 85
jetties 37, 58, 93, 94
Jumbo 22–24

K

Kean, David L. 49–51
Kean family 77–79, 91, 94, 98,
    107, 108, 110
Kechemeche tribe 14
Kelly family 77, 79, 91, 94, 98,
    107, 110

About the Authors

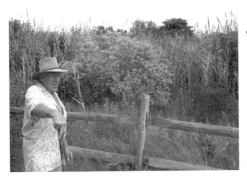

Joseph G. Burcher is one of the last surviving residents of South Cape May. His earliest memory of the borough dates to the mid-1920s, when he first visited his grandparents at the cottage built for them in 1923. Shortly afterward, Joe began spending all his summer months as a child and young adult in South Cape May, up through the early 1940s, when he joined the U.S. Navy. Joe's father, Edgar F. Burcher Sr., was South Cape May's last borough clerk, serving from 1941 to 1945. Two homes owned by members of the Burcher family were among the last left standing in South Cape May in the early 1950s. An alumnus of Temple University, where he earned a master of arts in education, Joe is an associate professor emeritus of the College of New Jersey. His active career at the college spanned three decades and focused on early childhood education. Since 1952, Joe has spent his summers at his cottage in West Cape May on Sunset Boulevard, overlooking the original site of South Cape May.

R obert Kenselaar has been on the staff of the New York Public Library since 1982, starting as a music librarian, then working as a research collection development specialist and now serving in its Development Office. His library experience also includes work with local history collections while on the staff of the Newark (New Jersey) Public Library, in addition to serving as assistant curator of the Rutgers University Institute of Jazz Studies. He has served on the writing staff of the *Aquarian Weekly*, and his other publications include articles in the Rutgers *Annual Review of Jazz Studies*, the *New Grove Dictionary of American Music* and *Cape May Magazine*. He holds a master of arts in American civilization from New York University and a master of library service from Rutgers University.